THE LEGEND OF SLEEPY HOLLOW.

A pleasing land of drowsy head it was,
Of dreams that wave before the half-shut eye;
And of gay castles in the clouds that pass,
For ever flushing round a summer sky.
CASTLE OF INDOLENCE.

In the bosom of one of the spacious coves which indent the eastern shore of the Hudson, at that broad expansion of the river denominated by the ancient Dutch navigators the Tappaan Zee, and where they always prudently shortened sail, and implored the protection of St. Nicholas when they crossed, there lies a small market-town or rural port, which by some is called Greensburgh, but which is more generally and properly known by the name of Tarry Town. This name was given, we are told, in former days, by the good housewives of the adjacent country, from the inveterate propensity of their husbands to linger about the village tavern on market days. Be that as it may, I do not vouch for the fact, but merely advert to it, for the sake of being precise and authentic. Not far from this village, perhaps about three miles, there is a little valley, or rather lap of land among high hills, which is one of the quietest places in the whole world. A small brook glides through it, with just murmur enough to lull one to repose; and the occasional whistle of a quail, or tapping of a woodpecker, is almost the only sound that ever breaks in upon the uniform tranquillity.

Washington Irving

✳ ✳ ✳

THE LEGEND
OF
SLEEPY HOLLOW.

———•———

DIE SAGE
VON
SLEEPY HOLLOW.

Impressum:

© 2020 Maria Weber (Hrsg. u. Bearb.)
Deutsche Textgrundlage nach der Übersetzung von
W. A. Lindau, Dresden 1822
Herstellung und Verlag: BoD – Books on Demand, Norderstedt.
ISBN: 978-3- 75281-375-3

DIE SAGE VON SLEEPY HOLLOW.

Ein entzückend träges Land war's,
Wo Traumbilder vorm halb geschloß'nen Aug',
Und am azurnen Himmel in stetem Strome
Wolkenschlösser vorüberziehen.
CASTLE OF INDOLENCE.

In einer der weiten Buchten, welche in das östliche Gestade des Hudson einlaufen, bei jener Ausdehnung des Flußbettes, die von den alten holländischen Seefahrern der *Tappaan-Zee* genannt wurde, wo sie immer vorsichtig die Segel einzogen und den Schutz des heiligen Nikolaus anriefen, wenn sie überfuhren – liegt ein kleiner Marktflecken, ein Hafendorf, von einigen Greensburgh genannt, allgemeiner aber unter dem Namen *Tarrytown*[1] bekannt. Diesen Namen sollen in früheren Zeiten die guten Hausfrauen in der Umgegend aufgebracht haben, weil unter ihren Männern die eingewurzelte Gewohnheit herrschte, an Markttagen in der Dorfschenke zu verweilen. Sei dem wie ihm wolle, ich verbürge die Tatsache nicht, sondern berühre sie bloß, um genau und glaubwürdig zu sein. Nicht weit, ungefähr anderthalb Stunden Weges vom Dorfe, liegt ein kleines Tal, oder vielmehr ein Fleckchen Land zwischen hohen Bergen, eines der ruhigsten Plätzchen in der ganzen Welt. Ein kleiner Bach durchfließt es, und murmelt gerade genug, um jemanden in Schlaf zu lullen, und das gelegentliche Pfeifen einer Wachtel oder das Geschrei eines Spechts sind fast die einzigen Töne, die je die einförmige Ruhe unterbrechen.

---

[1] „Zauderstadt.“

I recollect that, when a stripling, my first exploit in squirrel shooting was in a grove of tall walnut trees that shades one side of the valley. I had wandered into it at noon time, when all nature is peculiarly quiet, and was startled by the roar of my own gun, as it broke the sabbath still ness around, and was prolonged and reverberated by the angry echoes. If ever I should wish for a retreat, whither I might steal from the world and its distractions, and dream quietly away the remnant of a troubled life, I know of none more promising than this little valley.

From the listless repose of the place, and the peculiar character of its inhabitants, who are descendants from the original Dutch settlers, this sequestered glen has long been known by the name of SLEEPY HOLLOW, and its rustic lads are called the Sleepy Hollow Boys throughout all the neighbouring country. A drowsy, dreamy influence seems to hang over the land, and to pervade the very atmosphere. Some say that the place was bewitched by a high German doctor during the early days of the settlement; others, that an old Indian chief, the prophet or wizard of his tribe, held his powwows there before the country was discovered by Master Hendrick Hudson. Certain it is, the place still continues under the sway of some witching power, that holds a spell over the minds of the good people, causing them to walk in a continual reverie. They are given to all kinds of marvellous beliefs; are subject to trances and visions; and frequently see strange sights, and hear music and voices in the air.

Ich erinnere mich, daß ich als Knabe meinen ersten Versuch in der Eichhörnchenjagd in einem Wäldchen von hohen Walnußbäumen machte, die eine Seite jenes Tales beschatten. Ich war um die Mittagszeit dahin gewandert, wo in der Natur eine eigene Stille herrscht, und stutzte über den lauten Knall meiner Flinte, der die Sabbatstille ringsumher brach, und lange vom zürnenden Widerhall zurückgeworfen wurde. Sollte ich je eine Zuflucht wünschen, wohin ich mich von der Welt und ihren Zerstreuungen zurückziehen könnte, um den verbliebenen Rest eines bewegten Lebens ruhig zu verträumen, so wüßte ich keines, das mehr verspräche, als dieses kleine Tal.

Die träge Ruhe des Ortes und die eigene Gemütsart seiner Bewohner, die von den ursprünglichen niederländischen Ansiedlern abstammen, haben dem einsamen Tal vor langer Zeit den Namen *Sleepy Hollow*[2], eingebracht, und die jungen Landleute, die es bewohnen, heißen überall in der Umgegend die *Sleepy-Hollow-Jungen*. Ein schläfriger, verträumter Einfluß scheint über dem Land zu walten und die Atmosphäre zu durchdringen. Einige sagen, ein deutscher Arzt hätte das Tal in der frühesten Zeit der Ansiedelung bezaubert, andere wollen, es hätte ein alter Indianerhäuptling, der Wahrsager oder Zauberer seines Stammes, hier seine Künste getrieben, ehe Master Hendrick Hudson das Land entdeckte. So viel ist gewiß, daß der Ort immer noch unter dem Einfluß einer gewissen Zaubergewalt steht, die die Gedanken der guten Leute in ihren Bann zieht und sie dazu bringt, in ständiger Träumerei zu wandeln. Sie hängen jeder Art von Wunderglauben nach; unterliegen Trancen und Visionen, sehen oft seltsame Erscheinungen, hören Musik und Stimmen in der Luft.

---

[2] Anm. d. Hrsg.: „Schläfrige Senke."

The whole neighbourhood abounds with local tales, haunted spots, and twilight superstitions; stars shoot and meteors glare oftener across the valley than in any other part of the country; and the nightmare, with her whole nine fold, seems to make it the favourite scene of her gambols.

The dominant spirit, however, that haunts this enchanted region, and seems to be commander in chief of all the powers of the air, is the apparition of a figure on horseback without a head. It is said by some to be the ghost of a Hessian trooper, whose head had been carried away by a cannon ball, in some nameless battle during the revolutionary war; and who is ever and anon seen by the country folk, hurrying along in the gloom of night, as if on the wings of the wind. His haunts are not confined to the valley, but extend at times to the adjacent roads, and especially to the vicinity of a church that is at no great distance. Indeed, certain of the most authentic historians of those parts, who have been careful in collecting and collating the floating facts concerning this spectre, allege that, the body of the trooper having been buried in the churchyard, the ghost rides forth to the scene of battle in nightly quest of his head; and that the rushing speed with which he sometimes passes along the Hollow, like a midnight blast, is owing to his being belated, and in a hurry to get back to the churchyard before day-break.

Such is the general purport of this legendary superstition, which has furnished materials for many a wild story in that region of shadows; and the spectre is known, at all the country firesides, by the name of the Headless Horseman of Sleepy Hollow.

Die ganze Umgegend ist voll von örtlichen Märchen, Spukgeschichten und Zwielicht-Aberglauben; Lufterscheinungen und Sternschnuppen ziehen öfter leuchtend über das Tal, als in anderen Teilen der Gegend, und der Alp mit seinem Gefolge scheint es zum Lieblingsschauplatz seiner Gaukeleien erkoren zu haben.

Der herrschende Geist dieses bezauberten Gebietes aber, der Oberfeldherr gleichsam aller luftigen Mächte, ist die Gestalt eines Reiters ohne Kopf. Einige sagen, es sei der Geist eines hessischen Reiters, dem in irgendeinem namenlosen Gefecht während des Freiheitkrieges eine Kanonenkugel den Kopf weggerissen hätte, und der nun immerfort von den Landleuten gesehen wird, wie er bei nächtlichem Dunkel wie auf den Flügeln des Windes dahin eilt. Sein Spuk ist nicht auf das Tal beschränkt, und erstreckt sich zuweilen auf die benachbarten Straßen, und besonders in die Gegend einer nicht weit entfernten Kirche. Die glaubwürdigsten Geschichtschreiber dieser Gegenden, welche die zerstreuten Sagen über dieses Gespenst sorgfältig gesammelt und verglichen haben, melden allerdings, der Reiter, dessen Leib auf dem Kirchhofe begraben worden sei, reite allnächtlich auf das Schlachtfeld, um seinen Kopf zu suchen, und wenn er zuweilen wie ein mitternächtlicher Windstoß durch das Tal fahre, habe er sich verspätet, und habe es eilig, vor Tagesanbruch zum Kirchhof zurückzukehren.

Dies ist es, was der Aberglaube zu erzählen weiß, und was den Stoff zu mancher seltsamen Geschichte in diesem Schattengebiete gegeben hat. An jedem ländlichen Herd in der ganzen Gegend ist das Gespenst als „der kopflose Reiter von Sleepy Hollow" bekannt.

It is remarkable that the visionary propensity I have mentioned is not confined to the native in habitants of the valley, but is unconsciously imbibed by everyone who resides there for a time. However wide awake they may have been before they entered that sleepy region, they are sure, in a little time, to inhale the witching influence of the air, and begin to grow imaginative—to dream dreams, and see apparitions.

I mention this peaceful spot with all possible laud; for it is in such little retired Dutch valleys, found here and there embosomed in the great state of New York, that population, manners, and customs, remain fixed; while the great torrent of migration and improvement, which is making such incessant changes in other parts of this restless country, sweeps by them unobserved. They are like those little nooks of still water which border a rapid stream; where we may see the straw and bubble riding quietly at anchor, or slowly revolving in their mimic harbour, undisturbed by the rush of the passing current. Though many years have elapsed since I trod the drowsy shades of Sleepy Hollow, yet I question whether I should not still find the same trees and the same families vegetating in its sheltered bosom.

In this by-place of nature there abode, in a remote period of American history, that is to say, some thirty years since, a worthy wight of the name of Ichabod Crane; who sojourned, or, as he expressed it, "tarried," in Sleepy Hollow, for the purpose of instructing the children of the vicinity.

Es ist bemerkenswert, daß der erwähnte Hang zum zweiten Gesichte nicht bloß den eingeborenen Bewohnern des Tales eigen ist, sondern unbewußt von jedem eingesogen wird, der sich eine Zeitlang darin aufhält. Wie munter er auch gewesen sein mag, bevor er das schläfrige Gebiet betrat, er wird gewiß in kurzer Zeit dem bezaubernden Einfluß der Luft erliegen und beginnen, seltsame Träume zu träumen und Erscheinungen sehen.

Ich will übrigens dieses friedlichen Plätzchens mit allem möglichen Lob erwähnen; denn in diesen abgelegenen niederländischen Tälern, die man hier und da im großen Staat New York findet, bleiben Bewohner, Sitten und Gebräuche unverändert, während der große Strom der Menschenwanderung und der Fortschritt, der so unablässige Veränderungen in anderen Teilen dieses rastlos strebenden Landes hervorbringt, unbemerkt an ih-nen vorübergeht. Sie gleichen jenen kleinen Buchten stillen Wassers, die an reißende Ströme grenzen, wo der Strohhalm und die Luftblase ruhig im Wasser liegen, oder sich langsam in der hafenähnlichen Bucht drehen, ungestört von der ungestüm vorüberrauschenden Flut. Viele Jahre sind zwar verflossen, seit ich die einlullenden Schatten von Sleepy Hollow betrat, und ich frage mich, ob ich noch immer dieselben Bäume und dieselben Bewohner in dem geschirmten Schoße des Tales ihr Scheinleben fortsetzen sehen würde.

In diesem Schlupfwinkel der Natur wohnte, in einem lange zurückliegenden Zeitraum der amerikanischen Geschichte, das heißt, vor etwas mehr als dreißig Jahren, ein wackerer Mann namens Ichabod Crane, welcher sich in Sleepy Hollow aufhielt, oder, wie er sagte, dort *zauderte*, um die Kinder der Umgegend zu unterrichten.

He was a native of Connecticut: a state which supplies the Union with pioneers for the mind as well as for the forest, and sends forth yearly its legions of frontier woodmen and country school masters. The cognomen of Crane was not inapplicable to his person. He was tall, but exceedingly lank, with narrow shoulders, long arms and legs, hands that dangled a mile out of his sleeves, feet that might have served for shovels, and his whole frame most loosely hung together. His head was small, and flat at top, with huge ears, large green glassy eyes, and a long snipe nose, so that it looked like a weathercock, perched upon his spindle neck, to tell which way the wind blew. To see him striding along the profile of a hill on a windy day, with his clothes bagging and fluttering about him, one might have mistaken him for the genius of famine descending upon the earth, or some scarecrow eloped from a cornfield.

His school-house was a low building of one large room, rudely constructed of logs; the windows partly glazed, and partly patched with leaves of old copy books. It was most ingeniously secured at vacant hours, by a withe twisted in the handle of the door, and stakes set against the window shutters; so that, though a thief might get in with perfect ease, he would find some embarrassment in getting out; an idea most probably borrowed by the architect, Yost Van Houten, from the mystery of an eelpot.

Er stammte aus Connecticut, einem Staat, der die vereinigten Staaten mit Pionieren sowohl für den Geist, wie auch für den Wald versorgt, und jährlich ganze Scharen von Holzfällern und Landschullehrern aussendet. Der Name *Crane*[3] paßte nicht übel zu seiner Gestalt. Er war hoch gewachsen, aber ungemein dünn, mit schmalen Schultern, langen Armen und Beinen, Händen, die eine Meile aus seinen Ärmeln baumelten, Füßen, die zu Schaufeln hätten dienen können, und seine Gliedmaßen schlackerten an seinem Körper. Sein Kopf war klein und oben abgeflacht, mit ungeheuren Ohren, großen, wäßrig grünen Augen, einer langen spitzen Schnepfennase, und das Ganze sah aus wie ein Wetterhahn, der auf dem Spindelhalse saß, um anzusagen, woher der Wind wehte. Wenn man ihn an einem windigen Tage längs dem Rande eines Hügels hinschreiten sah, und die Kleider wie ein Sack um ihn flatterten, hätte man ihn für den Genius des Hungers halten können, der auf die Erde hinabstieg, oder für eine aus dem Feld entlaufene Vogelscheuche.

Sein Schulhaus war ein niedriges Gebäude, das einen einzigen großen Raum enthielt, und nur plump aus Balken zusammen gesetzt war; die Fenster waren teils verglast, teils mit Blättern alter Schreibhefte verklebt. In Freistunden war es sehr sinnreich durch eine in den Türgriff geflochtene Weidenrute, und Pfähle, die gegen die Fensterladen gestellt waren, verwahrt, so daß ein Dieb sehr leicht hätte hereinkommen können, aber einige Schwierigkeit gefunden haben würde, wieder hinauszukommen; eine Idee, die vom Architekten Yost Van Houten wahrscheinlich aus der Konstruktion einer Aalreuse entlehnt wurde.

---

[3] „Kranich."

The school-house stood in a rather lonely but pleasant situation, just at the foot of a woody hill, with a brook running close by, and a formidable birch tree growing at one end of it. From hence the low murmur of his pupils' voices, conning over their lessons, might be heard in a drowsy summer's day, like the hum of a bee-hive; interrupted now and then by the authoritative voice of the master, in the tone of menace or command; or, peradventure, by the appalling sound of the birch, as he urged some tardy loiterer along the flowery path of knowledge. Truth to say, he was a conscientious man, that ever bore in mind the golden maxim, "Spare the rod and spoil the child."—Ichabod Crane's scholars certainly were not spoiled.

I would not have it imagined, however, that he was one of those cruel potentates of the school, who joy in the smart of their subjects; on the contrary, he administered justice with discrimination rather than severity; taking the burthen off the backs of the weak, and laying it on those of the strong. Your mere puny stripling, that winced at the least flourish of the rod, was passed by with indulgence; but the claims of justice were satisfied, by inflicting a double portion on some little, tough, wrong-headed, broad-skirted Dutch urchin, who sulked and swelled and grew dogged and sullen beneath the birch. All this he called "doing his duty by their parents;" and he never inflicted a chastisement without following it by the assurance, so consolatory to the smarting urchin, that "he would remember it and thank him for it the longest day he had to live."

Das Schulhaus hatte eine einsame, aber ziemlich angenehme Lage, am Fuße eines waldigen Hügels, nahe an einem Bach, und war von einer gewaltigen Birke beschattet. Von dort konnte man an einem schläfrigen Sommertage das dumpfe Gemurmel der Stimmen seiner Schüler, wenn sie ihre Aufgaben lernten, wie das Summen eines Bienenschwarmes hören, nur zuweilen unterbrochen von der respektgebietenden Stimme des Lehrers, oder vielleicht von dem furchtbaren Ton der Rute, wenn er einen Faulenzer auf dem blumigen Pfad des Wissens antrieb. Man muß es der Wahrheit gemäß gestehen, er war ein gewissenhafter Mann, der immer an den goldenen Spruch dachte: „Sparst du die Rute, so verhätschelst du das Kind." Ichabod Cranes Schüler wurden gewiß nicht verhätschelt.

Nun denke man aber nicht, er hätte zu jenen grausamen Schulgebietern gehört, die am Leid der Untertanen Freude finden; nein, er verwaltete die Gerechtigkeit eher mit gehöriger Unterscheidung, als mit Strenge, nahm die Bürde von den Schultern des Schwachen und legte sie dem Starken auf. Ein mageres Bürschlein, das schon beim bloßen Anblick der Rute winselte, wurde nachsichtig behandelt; aber die Ansprüche der Gerechtigkeit wurden befriedigt, indem der zähe, starrköpfige, stämmige niederländische Bube, der unter der Rute trotzte und zürnte, und mürrisch und verbissen wurde, eine doppelte Abreibung erhielt. Alles dies nannte er, „seine Pflicht für die Eltern tun", und nie fügte er eine Züchtigung zu, ohne die für den leidenden Knaben so tröstliche Versicherung hinzuzufügen, der Gestrafte werde „daran gedenken und es ihm sein Leben lang danken".

When school hours were over, he was even the companion and playmate of the larger boys; and on holyday afternoons would convoy some of the smaller ones home, who happened to have pretty sisters, or good housewives for mothers, noted for the comforts of the cupboard. Indeed it behoved him to keep on good terms with his pupils. The revenue arising from his school was small, and would have been scarcely sufficient to furnish him with daily bread, for he was a huge feeder, and though lank, had the dilating powers of an Anaconda; but to help out his maintenance, he was, according to country custom in those parts, boarded and lodged at the houses of the farmers, whose children he instructed. With these he lived successively a week at a time; thus going the rounds of the neighbourhood, with all his worldly effects tied up in a cotton handkerchief.

That all this might not be too onerous on the purses of his rustic patrons, who are apt to consider the costs of schooling a grievous burthen, and schoolmasters as mere drones, he had various ways of rendering himself both useful and agreeable. He assisted the farmers occasionally in the lighter labours of their farms; helped to make hay; mended the fences; took the horses to water; drove the cows from pasture; and cut wood for the winter fire. He laid aside, too, all the dominant dignity and absolute sway with which he lorded it in his little empire, the school, and became wonderfully gentle and ingratiating. He found favour in the eyes of the mothers, by petting the children, particularly the youngest; and like the lion bold, which whilome so magnanimously the lamb did hold, he would sit with a child on one knee, and rock a cradle with his foot for whole hours together.

Nach den Schulstunden war er sogar der Gefährte und Spielgeselle der größeren Knaben, und an Feiertagsnachmittagen führte er Kleinere heim, die hübsche Schwestern hatten, oder deren Mütter gute Hausfrauen waren, die über einen gut gefüllten Vorratsschrank verfügten. Er war freilich in einer Lage, die es ihm gebot, mit seinen Schülern auf gutem Fuße zu stehen. Seine Einkünfte aus der Schule waren gering und hätten kaum ausgereicht, um ihn mit dem täglichen Brot zu versorgen, da er ein gewaltiger Esser war, und, wenn auch mager, doch die Kraft hatte, sich wie eine Anaconda auszudehnen; um ihm aber seinen Unterhalt zu erleichtern, erhielt er, nach der ländlichen Sitte in jenen Gegenden, in den Häusern der Bauern, deren Kinder er unterrichtete, Kost und Wohnung. So lebte er abwechselnd eine Woche bei jedem, und machte die Runde in der Umgegend, mit seinen sämtlichen Habseligkeiten in einem baumwollenen Tuch.

Er hatte verschiedene Mittel, sich nützlich und angenehm zu machen, damit die Kosten seiner Ernährung den Beuteln der ländlichen Gönner, die das Schulgeld für eine große Last und die Schulmeister für bloße Parasiten hielten, nicht zu lästig fallen sollten. Zuweilen leistete er den Bauern in leichten wirtschaftlichen Arbeiten Beistand, half beim Heumachen, besserte die Zäune aus, führte die Pferde zum Wasser, trieb die Kühe auf die Weide und sägte Holz zur Winterfeuerung. Er legte auch seine ganze gebieterische Würde und unbeschränkte Herrschaft, womit er in seinem kleinen Reiche, der Schule, waltete, beiseite, und wurde wunderbar freundlich und einschmeichelnd. In den Augen der Mütter fand er Gnade, wenn er die Kinder, zumal die Jüngsten, verhätschelte; und dem kühnen Löwen gleich, der zuweilen so großmütig das Lamm hält, saß er oft mit einem Kinde stundenlang auf dem Knie und stieß mit dem Fuße an eine Wiege.

In addition to his other vocations, he was the singing-master of the neighbourhood, and picked up many bright shillings by instructing the young folks in psalmody. It was a matter of no little vanity to him, on Sundays, to take his station in front of the church gallery, with a band of chosen singers; where, in his own mind, he completely carried away the palm from the parson. Certain it is, his voice resounded far above all the rest of the congregation; and there are peculiar quavers still to be heard in that church, and which may even be heard half a mile off, quite to the opposite side of the mill-pond, on a still Sunday morning, which are said to be legitimately descended from the nose of Ichabod Crane. Thus, by divers little makeshifts, in that ingenious way which is commonly denominated "by hook and by crook," the worthy pedagogue got on tolerably enough, and was thought, by all who understood nothing of the labour of headwork, to have a wonderful easy life of it.

The schoolmaster is generally a man of some importance in the female circle of a rural neighbourhood; being considered a kind of idle gentleman-like personage, of vastly superior taste and accomplishments to the rough country swains, and, indeed, inferior in learning only to the parson. His appearance, therefore, is apt to occasion some little stir at the tea-table of a farmhouse, and the addition of a supernumerary dish of cakes or sweet meats, or peradventure, the parade of a silver tea pot. Our man of letters, therefore, was peculiarly happy in the smiles of all the country damsels.

Zusätzlich zu seinen anderen Berufen, war er der Gesangslehrer der Umgegend, und strich so manchen blanken Schilling für den Unterricht im Psalmensingen ein. Er bildete sich nicht wenig darauf ein, wenn er an Sonntagen mit einer Anzahl erlesener Sänger seinen Platz dem Chore gegenüber nahm, wo er nach seiner Meinung einen vollständigen Sieg über den Pfarrer davontrug. So viel ist gewiß, seine Stimme überschrie jede andere in der Versammlung, und man hört in dieser Kirche noch immer ein zitterndes Beben, das man an einem stillen Sonntagmorgen gar eine Viertelstunde weit, auf der andern Seite des Mühlenteiches, noch vernimmt, und das man für einen Nachhall aus Ichabod Cranes Nase hält. Und so gelang es dem würdigen Schulmann, mithilfe verschiedener Mittel, welche man für gewöhnlich „auf Biegen und Brechen" nennt, sich leidlich durchzuschlagen, und wer nicht wußte, was es bedeutet, Kopfarbeit zu leisten, könnte meinen, er müßte ein ungemein einfaches Leben haben.

Der Schulmeister gilt in der Regel gewöhnlich für einen ziemlich wichtigen Mann in dem weiblichen Kreise der Dorfbewohner, und man hält ihn ein wenig für einen nicht arbeitenden Vornehmen, der den rohen Bauernburschen an Geschmack und Geist unendlich überlegen ist und in Gelehrsamkeit nur dem Pfarrer nachsteht. Sein Erscheinen bewirkte daher eine ungewöhnliche Bewegung am Teetisch in einem Pächterhaus, und es wurde ein Teller mit Kuchen oder Zuckerwerk mehr aufgetischt, oder vielleicht gar mit der silbernen Teekanne geprahlt. Unser Gelehrter hatte daher ein besonderes Glück, die lächelnden Blicke aller Landmädchen auf sich zu ziehen.

How he would figure among them in the churchyard, between services on Sundays gathering grapes for them from the wild vines that overrun the surrounding trees; reciting for their amusement all the epitaphs on the tombstones; or sauntering, with a whole bevy of them, along the banks of the adjacent mill-pond; while the more bashful country bumpkins hung sheepishly back, envying his superior elegance and address.

From his half itinerant life, also, he was a kind of travelling gazette, carrying the whole budget of local gossip from house to house; so that his appearance was always greeted with satisfaction. He was, moreover, esteemed by the women as a man of great erudition, for he had read several books quite through, and was a perfect master of Cotton Mather's History of New-England Witchcraft, in which, by the way, he most firmly and potently believed.

He was, in fact, an odd mixture of small shrewdness and simple credulity. His appetite for the marvellous, and his powers of digesting it, were equally extraordinary; and both had been in creased by his residence in this spell-bound region. No tale was too gross or monstrous for his capacious swallow. It was often his delight, after his school was dismissed in the afternoon, to stretch himself on the rich bed of clover, bordering the little brook that whimpered by his school-house, and there con over old Mather's direful tales, until the gathering dusk of the evening made the printed page a mere mist before his eyes.

Wie glänzte er an Sonntagen unter ihnen auf dem Kirchhof! Da pflückte er ihnen bald Trauben von den willden Reben, die sich um die umstehenden Bäume schlangen, las zu ihrer Unterhaltung alle Grabschriften auf den Leichensteinen, oder schlenderte mit einem ganzen Schwarm längs dem Mühlenteiche, während die ungebildeteren Bauerntölpel schüchtern hinterherschlichen und ihn um seine überlegene Feinheit und Eleganz beneideten.

Durch seine fast nomadische Lebensweise war er eine Art von wandernder Zeitung, und trug den ganzen Vorrat von Klatschgeschichten der Umgegend von Haus zu Haus, weshalb denn sein Erscheinen immer sehr willkommen war. Die Weiber schätzten ihn überdies als einen Mann von großer Gelehrsamkeit, da er mehre Bücher von Anfang bis Ende gelesen hatte und Cotton Mather's Geschichte der Hexerei in Neu-England vollkommen auswendig kannte, woran er übrigens steif und fest glaubte.

Er war in der Tat eine seltsame Mischung von etwas Verschlagenheit und einfältiger Leichtgläubigkeit. Sein Appetit auf das Wunderbare und seine Fähigkeit, es zu verdauen, waren gleichermaßen außerordentlich, und beide waren während seines Aufenthaltes in dem bezauberten Gebiet gewachsen. Kein Märchen war zu plump, zu ungeheuer für ihn, als daß er es nicht leicht verschlungen hätte. Nachmittags nach der Schulstunde machte er sich oft die Freude, sich auf dem üppigen Kleebett auszustrecken, am Ufer des Bächleins, das neben seinem Schulhause hinab rieselte, und sich dann in Mather's furchtbare Geschichten zu vertiefen, bis beim anbrechenden Abenddunkel die Buchstaben vor seinen Augen verschwammen.

Then, as he wended his way, by swamp and stream and awful woodland, to the farm-house where he happened to be quartered, every sound of nature, at that witching hour, fluttered his excited imagination: the moan of the whip-poor-will[4] from the hill side; the boding cry of the tree-toad, that harbinger of storm; the dreary hooting of the screech-owl; or the sudden rustling in the thicket of birds frightened from their roost. The fire flies, too, which sparkled most vividly in the darkest places, now and then startled him, as one of uncommon brightness would stream across his path; and if, by chance, a huge blockhead of a beetle came winging his blundering flight against him, the poor varlet was ready to give up the ghost, with the idea that he was struck with a witch's token. His only resource on such occasions, either to drown thought, or drive away evil spirits, was to sing psalm tunes;—and the good people of Sleepy Hollow, as they sat by their doors of an evening, were often filled with awe, at hearing his nasal melody, "in linked sweetness long drawn out," floating from the distant hill, or along the dusky road.

---

[4] The whip-poor-will is a bird which is only heard at night. It receives its name from its note, which is thought to resemble those words.

Ging er dann durch Sumpf und Strom und furcht-einflößende Wälder zu dem Gehöft, wo er gerade seinen Wohnsitz hatte, so regte jeder Laut in dieser bezauberten Stunde seine Phantasie an; der Klageton des Wipp-pur-will[5] vom Gebirge, das unheilverkündende Geschrei der Baum-kröte, der Vorbotin des Sturms; der trostlose Ruf der Nachteule, oder das plötzliche Flattern der Vögel im Dickicht, die in ihren Nestern aufgeschreckt wurden. Auch die Glühwürmchen, die zuweilen in den dunkelsten Stellen hell funkelten, erschreckten ihn, wenn ein ungewöhnlich hell glänzender über seinen Pfad flog, und wenn zufällig ein überaus dummer Käfer in ungeschicktem Fluge auf ihn stieß, so wollte der arme Kerl schier seinen Geist aufgeben, aus Angst, er wäre verzaubert worden. Das einzige Mittel, das ihm bei solchen Gelegenheiten einfiel, um die Gedanken zu unterdrücken oder die bösen Geister zu verjagen, war, Psalmen anzustimmen, und wenn die guten Leute von Sleepy Hollow abends vor ihren Türen saßen, wurden sie oft von Furcht ergriffen bei dem Schall seiner *„in langge-zogener Süße"*[6] erklingenden nasalen Töne, die von einem entfernten Hügel oder von der düsteren Straße herüber-wehten.

[5] Ein Vogel, der sich nur in der Nacht hören läßt, und den Na-men von dem Ton seines Rufes hat.
[6] Milton, *L'Allegro*.

Another of his sources of fearful pleasure was, to pass long winter evenings with the old Dutch wives, as they sat spinning by the fire, with a row of apples roasting and sputtering along the hearth, and listen to their marvellous tales of ghosts and goblins, and haunted fields, and haunted brooks, and haunted bridges, and haunted houses, and particularly of the headless horseman, or Galloping Hessian of the Hollow, as they sometimes called him. He would delight them equally by his anecdotes of witchcraft, and of the direful omens and portentous sights and sounds in the air, which prevailed in the earlier times of Connecticut; and would frighten them wofully with speculations upon comets and shooting stars; and with the alarming fact that the world did absolutely turn round, and that they were half the time topsy turvy!

But if there was a pleasure in all this, while snugly cuddling in the chimney corner of a chamber that was all of a ruddy glow from the crackling wood fire; and where, of course, no spectre dared to show its face, it was dearly purchased by the terrors of his subsequent walk homewards. What fearful shapes and shadows beset his path amidst the dim and ghastly glare of a snowy night !

With what wistful look did he eye every trembling ray of light streaming across the waste fields from some distant window!—How often was he appalled by some shrub covered with snow, which, like sheeted spectre, beset his very path!

Eine andere Quelle schaurigen Vergnügens war es für ihn, die langen Winterabende bei den alten niederländischen Weibern zuzubringen, wenn sie spinnend am Feuer saßen, und auf eine Schnur gereihte Äpfel knisternd am Herd trockneten. Er lauschte dann ihren wunderbaren Geschichten von Geistern und Kobolden, von verwünschten Feldern, Bächen, Brücken und Häusern, wo Gespenster umgingen, und besonders von dem kopflosen Reiter, oder dem galoppierenden Hessen aus der Senke, wie man ihn zuweilen nannte. Sie wiederum lauschten mit ebenso großem Vergnügen seinen Anekdoten von Zauberkünsten, schrecklichen Vorbedeutungen und unheilverkündenden Zeichen und Tönen in der Luft, wovon man in früheren Zeiten in Connecticut viel zu reden wußte, und er setzte sie in jämmerlichen Schrecken, wenn er ihnen seine Betrachtungen über Kometen und Sternschnuppen mitteilte, und von dem beunruhigenden Umstand sprach, daß die Welt sich ganz und gar herumdrehte, und die Menschen ihr halbes Leben lang Purzelbäume machten!

Doch wenn auch alles dies angenehm war, wenn er sich behaglich am Kamine in einer Stube wärmte, wo das knisternde Feuer einen rötlichen Glanz verbreitete, und gewiß kein Gespenst sich zu zeigen wagte, so wurde es durch die Schrecken, die ihn auf dem Heimweg verfolgten, teuer erstanden. Welche furchtbaren Gestalten und Schatten seinen Pfad bei dem trüben, grausigen Schimmer einer verschneiten Nacht besetzten!

Mit welchem sehnsuchtsvollen Blicke sah er auf jeden zitternden Lichtstrahl, der sich aus einem entfernten Fenster über das öde Gefilde ergoß! Wie oft erschreckte ihn ein beschneiter Busch, der sich wie ein weiß verhülltes Gespenst mitten auf seinem Pfade erhob!

How often did he shrink with curdling awe at the sound of his own steps on the frosty crust beneath his feet; and dread to look over his shoulder, lest he should behold some uncouth being tramping close behind him —and how often was he thrown into complete dismay by some rushing blast, howling among the trees, in the idea that it was the Galloping Hessian on one of his nightly scourings!

All these, however, were mere terrors of the night, phantoms of the mind that walk in darkness; and though he had seen many spectres in his time, and been more than once beset by Satan in divers shapes, in his lonely perambulations, yet daylight put an end to all these evils; and he would have passed a pleasant life of it, in despite of the Devil and all his works, if his path had not been crossed by a being that causes more perplexity to mortal man than ghosts, goblins, and the whole race of witches put together, and that was—a woman!

Among the musical disciples who assembled, one evening in each week, to receive his instructions in psalmody, was Katrina Van Tassel, the daughter and only child of a substantial Dutch farmer. She was a blooming lass of fresh eighteen; plump as a partridge; ripe and melting and rosy cheeked as one of her father's peaches, and universally famed, not merely for her beauty, but her vast expectations. She was withal a little of a coquette, as might be perceived even in her dress, which was a mixture of ancient and modern fashions, as most suited to set off her charms.

Wie oft erbebte er, vor Furcht erstarrend, bei dem Ton seiner eigenen Tritte auf der Frostdecke des Bodens, und scheute sich, über seine Schulter zu blicken, um nicht irgendein seltsames Wesen zu sehen, das dicht hinter ihm schreiten könnte! Wie oft war er außer sich vor Schrecken, wenn er bei einen Windstoße, der heulend durch die Bäume fuhr, den Hessen zu hören glaubte, der auf seinem nächtlichen Streifzug dahersprengte.

Doch alles dies waren nur nächtliche Schrecknisse, Spukgestalten, welche die im Finstern wandelnde Seele ergriffen, und wiewohl er viele Gespenster in seinem Leben gesehen hatte, und mehr als einmal auf seinen einsamen Wanderungen vom Satan in verschiedenen Gestalten angefallen worden war, so machte doch der Tag allen Übeln ein Ende, und er würde, trotz dem Teufel und seinen Werken, ein fröhliches Leben geführt haben, wenn nicht ein Wesen seinen Pfad durchkreuzt hätte, das die Menschen mehr verwirrt, als Gespenster, Kobolde und die ganze Sippschaft aller Hexen zusammen, und dies war – ein Weib.

Unter den Schülerinnen, die einmal wöchentlich Unterricht im Psalmensingen erhielten, war Katrina Van Tassel, das einzige Kind eines angesehenen niederländischen Gutsbesitzers. Sie war ein blühendes Mädchen, kaum achtzehn Jahre alt, drall wie ein Rebhuhn, reif, schmelzend und rosenwangig wie einer von ihres Vaters Pfirsichen, und allgemein berühmt, nicht bloß ihrer Reize, sondern auch ihrer großen Aussichten wegen. Sie war bei alledem ein wenig gefallsüchtig, was selbst ihre Kleider verrieten, die ein Gemisch von alter und neuer Sitte waren, wie es am besten paßte, um ihre Reize hervorzuheben.

She wore the ornaments of pure yellow gold, which her great-great-grandmother had brought over from Saardam; the tempting stomacher of the olden time; and withal a provokingly short petticoat, to display the prettiest foot and ankle in the country round.

Ichabod Crane had a soft and foolish heart to ward the sex; and it is not to be wondered at, that so tempting a morsel soon found favour in his eyes; more especially after he had visited her in her paternal mansion. Old Baltus Van Tassel was a perfect picture of a thriving, contented, liberal hearted farmer. He seldom, it is true, sent either his eyes or his thoughts beyond the boundaries of his own farm; but within those everything was snug, happy, and well-conditioned. He was satisfied with his wealth, but not proud of it; and piqued himself upon the hearty abundance, rather than the style in which he lived. His strong hold was situated on the banks of the Hudson, in one of those green, sheltered, fertile nooks, in which the Dutch farmers are so fond of nestling.

A great elm-tree spread its broad branches over it; at the foot of which bubbled up a spring of the softest and sweetest water, in a little well, formed of a barrel; and then stole sparkling away through the grass, to a neighbouring brook, that babbled along among elders and dwarf willows. Hard by the farm-house was a vast barn, that might have served for a church; every window and crevice of which seemed bursting forth with the treasures of the farm.

Sie trug Schmuck aus reinem Gold, die ihre Ur-Urgroß-
mutter aus Saardam mitgebracht hatte; das verführerische
Mieder aus der alten Zeit, und dazu ein recht ärgerlich kur-
zes Röckchen, um den hübschesten Fuß und Knöchel der
ganzen Gegend zu zeigen.

Ichabod Cranes weiches Herz war ganz vernarrt in die
Weiber, und es ist nicht zu verwundern, daß ein so verlok-
kender Bissen bald Gnade in seinen Augen fand, insbeson-
dere, nachdem er ihres Vaters Haus besucht hatte. Der alte
Baltus Van Tassel war ein vollkommenes Bild eines blü-
henden, zufriedenen und edelherzigen Landmannes. Er ließ
freilich seine Augen selten über die Grenzen seines Land-
gutes hinaus wandern, aber innerhalb dieser Grenzen war
alles behaglich, glücklich und wohlgeordnet. Er war zufrie-
den mit seinem Reichtum, aber nicht stolz darauf, und
ärgerte sich mehr über den tüchtigen Überfluß, den er be-
saß, als über seine Lebensweise. Sein Sitz lag am Ufer des
Hudson, auf einem jener grünen, wohl geschirmten,
fruchtbaren Fleckchen, wo die niederländischen Landbau-
ern sich so gern einnisten.

Das Haus wurde von den breiten mächtigen Zweigen
eines alten Ulmenbaumes überschattet, an dessen Fuß ein
Quell des mildesten und süßesten Wassers entsprang, in
einen Brunnen, der aus einem Faß gebildet war, sprudelte,
und sich dann schimmernd durch das Gras zu einem nahen
Bache stahl, der geschwätzig zwischen Fliederbüschen und
Zwergweiden hinabrann. Dicht bei dem Wohnhaus stand
eine große Scheune, die zu einer Kirche hätte dienen können, wo aus jedem Fenster und jeder Spalte die Schätze des
Hofes hervorzudringen schienen.

The flail was busily resounding within it from morning to night; swallows and martins skimmed twittering about the eaves; and rows of pigeons, some with one eye turned up, as if watching the weather, some with their heads under their wings, or buried in their bosoms, and others swelling, and cooing, and bowing about their dames, were enjoying the sunshine on the roof. Sleek unwieldy porkers were grunting in the repose and abundance of their pens; from whence sallied forth, now and then, troops of sucking pigs, as if to snuff the air. A stately squadron of snowy geese were riding in an adjoining pond, convoying whole fleets of ducks; regiments of turkeys were gobbling through the farm-yard, and guinea fowls fretting about it, like ill-tempered housewives, with their peevish discontented cry. Before the barn door strutted the gallant cock, that pattern of a husband, a warrior, and a fine gentleman; clapping his burnished wings, and crowing in the pride and gladness of his heart—sometimes tearing up the earth with his feet, and then generously calling his ever-hungry family of wives and children to enjoy the rich morsel which he had discovered.

The pedagogue's mouth watered, as he looked upon this sumptuous promise of luxurious winter fare. In his devouring mind's eye, he pictured to himself every roasting pig running about with a pudding in its belly, and an apple in its mouth; the pigeons were snugly put to bed in a comfortable pie, and tucked in with a coverlet of crust; the geese were swimming in their own gravy; and the ducks pairing cosily in dishes, like snug married couples, with a decent competency of onion sauce.

Hier schallte von Morgen bis in die Nacht der geschäftige Dreschflegel; Schwalben nisteten zwitschernd längs der Traufe, und auf dem Dach sonnten sich Reihen von Tauben, wovon einige mit einem Auge aufblickten, als hätten sie das Wetter beobachtet, andere den Kopf unter den Flügeln oder auf der Brust verbargen, andere sich aufplusterten, gurrten und ihre Weibchen umwarben. Gepflegte, schwerfällige Mastschweine grunzten bei Ruhe und Überfluß in ihren Koben, woraus zuweilen Haufen von Ferkeln kamen, als hätten sie Luft schöpfen wollen. Eine stattliche Schaar schneeweißer Gänse schwamm in einem nahen Teich, und geleitete ganze Geschwader von Enten; Heere von Putern ließen ihren Ruf im Hof ertönen, und Perlhühner gingen unruhig hin und her, wie keifende Hausfrauen, mit ihrem mürrischen, verdrießlichen Geschrei. Vor dem Scheunentor prahlte der verliebte Hahn, das Muster eines Ehemannes, eines Kriegers und eines feinen Herrn, seine glänzenden Flügel schlagend, im Stolz und in der Freude seines Herzens krähend, und zuweilen die Erde aufscharrend, worauf er denn großmütig die ewig hungrigen Weiber und Kinder herbeirief, damit sich diese des entdeckten köstlichen Bissens erfreuen konnten.

Dem Schulmann lief das Wasser im Munde zusammen, als er auf diese herrliche Verheißung einer üppigen Winterkost blickte. Vor den Augen seiner gierigen Seele standen schon alle Spanferkel gebraten mit einem Kloß im Bauch und einem Apfel im Maul; die Tauben wurden wohlverwahrt in eine hübsche Pastete gebettet und mit einer Teigkruste bedeckt; die Gänse schwammen in ihrem eigenen Fette, und die Enten lagen paarweise in den Schüsseln, wie traulich verbundene Gatten, mit einer gehörigen Zutat von Zwiebelsauce.

In the porkers he saw carved out the future sleek side of bacon, and juicy relishing ham; not a turkey, but he beheld daintily trussed up, with its gizzard under its wing, and, peradventure, a necklace of savoury sausages; and even bright chanticleer himself lay sprawling on his back, in a side dish, with uplifted claws, as if craving that quarter, which his chivalrous spirit disdained to ask while living.

As the enraptured Ichabod fancied all this, and as he rolled his great green eyes over the fat meadow lands, the rich fields of wheat, of rye, of buck-wheat, and Indian corn, and the orchards burthened with ruddy fruit, which surrounded the warm tenement of Van Tassel, his heart yearned after the damsel who was to inherit these domains, and his imagination expanded with the idea, how they might be readily turned into cash, and the money invested in immense tracts of wild land, and shingle palaces in the wilderness. Nay, his busy fancy already realized his hopes, and presented to him the blooming Katrina, with a whole family of children, mounted on the top of a waggon loaded with household trumpery, with pots and kettles dangling beneath; and he beheld himself bestriding a pacing mare, with a colt at her heels, setting out for Kentucky, Tennessee, or the Lord knows where!

When he entered the house the conquest of his heart was complete. It was one of those spacious farm-houses, with high ridged, but lowly-sloping roofs, built in the style handed down from the first Dutch settlers. The low projecting eaves formed a piazza along the front, capable of being closed up in bad weather.

Aus den Mastschweinen sah er schon die glatte Speckseite und den saftigen, schmackhaften Schinken geschnitten, jeden Truthahn, köstlich zubereitet, mit dem Magen unter dem Flügel, und wohl auch mit einem Halsband aus köstlichen Bratwürsten; und selbst der glänzende Hahn lag als eine Beilage zappelnd auf dem Rücken, mit emporgehobenen Klauen, als hätte er um die Schonung gebeten, die sein ritterlicher Geist bei Lebzeiten zu erbitten verschmähte.

Als diese Bilder vor Ichabods entzückter Seele standen, als er seine großen grünen Augen über die fetten Wiesenäcker, die reichen Felder mit Weizen, Roggen, Buchweizen und Mais gleiten ließ, und die mit goldgelben Früchten beladenen Obstgärten betrachtete, die Van Tassels freundliche Besitzung umgaben, verlangte sein Herz nach der Jungfrau, welche diese Güter erben sollte, und seine Seele erhob sich bei dem Gedanken, wie schnell sie sich versilbern, und für das Geld ungeheure öde Landstriche und Schindelpaläste in der Wildnis ankaufen ließen. Ja, schon hatte seine geschäftige Seele diese Hoffnungen belebt, und er sah die blühende Katrina mit einem Häuflein von Kindern oben auf einem mit Hausgeräte beladenen Wagen, woran Töpfe und Kessel baumelten, und sich selber auf einer gemächlich schreitenden Stute, mit einem nachziehenden Fohlen, um nach Kentucky, Tennessee, oder Gott weiß wohin, zu wandern!

Er betrat das Haus, und die Eroberung seines Herzens war vollendet. Es war eines jener geräumigen Bauernhäuser mit hohen, leicht geneigten Dächern, die im Stil der ersten niederländischen Siedler erbaut wurden. Die weit überhängende Traufe bildete eine an der Frontseite verlaufende Veranda, die bei schlechtem Wetter verschlossen werden konnte.

Under this were hung flails, harness, various utensils of husbandry, and nets for fishing in the neighbouring river. Benches were built along the sides for summer use; and a great spinning wheel at one end, and a churn at the other, showed the various uses to which this important porch might be devoted. From this piazza the wondering Ichabod entered the hall, which formed the centre of the mansion, and the place of usual residence. Here, rows of resplendent pewter, ranged on a long dresser, dazzled his eyes. In one corner stood a huge bag of wool ready to be spun; in another a quantity of linsey woolsey just from the loom; ears of Indian corn, and strings of dried apples and peaches, hung in gay festoons along the walls, mingled with the gaud of red peppers; and a door left ajar gave him a peep into the best parlour, where the claw footed chairs, and dark mahogany tables, shone like mirrors; andirons, with their accompanying shovel and tongs, glistened from their covert of asparagus tops: mock oranges and conch shells decorated the mantel-piece; strings of various coloured birds' eggs were suspended above it; a great ostrich egg was hung from the centre of the room, and a corner cupboard, knowingly left open, displayed immense treasures of old silver and well mended china.

From the moment Ichabod laid his eyes upon these regions of delight, the peace of his mind was at an end, and his only study was how to gain the affections of the peerless daughter of Van Tassel.

Hier hingen Dreschflegel, Pferdegeschirr, verschiedene landwirtschaftliche Geräte, und Netze zum Fischen im nahen Flusse. Bänke waren auf den Seiten für den Sommer angebracht; ein großes Spinnrad an dem einen Ende und ein Butterfaß am andern zeigten, von welchem vielfältigen Nutzen dieser Gang sein konnte. Von dieser Veranda trat der staunende Ichabod in den Saal, der die Mitte des Hauses bildete und der gewöhnliche Aufenthalt der Bewohner war. Reihen von glänzendem Zinn, auf einem langen Anrichtetische aufgestellt, blendeten seine Augen. In einer Ecke stand ein ungeheurer Sack mit Wolle zum Spinnen, in einer anderen halbwollenes Zeug frisch vom Webstuhl; Maiskolben und Schnüre von getrockneten Äpfeln und Pfirsichen hingen neben aufgereihten roten Pfefferonen munter längs den Wänden. Durch die halb offene Türe blickte Ichabod in die gute Stube, wo Stühle mit Klauenfüßen und dunkle Mahagonitische wie Spiegel glänzten. Feuerböcke nebst Schaufeln und Zangen schimmerten unter ihrer Decke von Spargelköpfen; künstliche Pomeranzen und Muschelschalen schmückten den Kaminsims, Schnüre von vielfarbigen Vogeleiern waren darüber aufgehängt, ein großes Straußenei hing in des Zimmers Mitte, und ein absichtlich offen gelassener Schrank in der Ecke zeigte unermeßliche Schätze von altem Silber und wohl geflicktem Porzellan.

Es war um Ichabods Seelenfrieden geschehen, als er seinen Blick in dieses Gebiet der Wonne geworfen hatte, und sein einziges Trachten war nun dahin gerichtet, die Zuneigung der unvergleichlichen Tochter Van Tassels zu gewinnen.

In this enterprise, however, he had more real difficulties than generally fell to the lot of a knight errant of yore, who seldom had anything but giants, enchanters, fiery dragons, and such like easily conquered adversaries, to contend with; and had to make his way merely through gates of iron and brass, and walls of adamant, to the castle keep, where the lady of his heart was confined; all which he achieved as easily as a man would carve his way to the centre of a Christmas pie, and then the lady gave him her hand as a matter of course. Ichabod, on the contrary, had to win his way to the heart of a country coquette, beset with a labyrinth of whims and caprices, which were forever presenting new difficulties and impediments: and he had to encounter a host of fearful adversaries of real flesh and blood, the numerous rustic admirers, who beset every portal to her heart; keeping a watchful and angry eye upon each other, but ready to fly out in the common cause against any new competitor.

Among these the most formidable was a burly, roaring, roystering blade, of the name of Abraham, or, according to the Dutch abbreviation, Brom Van Brunt, the hero of the country round, which rung with his feats of strength and hardihood. He was broad-shouldered and double-jointed, with short curly black hair, and a bluff, but not unpleasant countenance, having a mingled air of fun and arrogance. From his Herculean fame and great powers of limb, he had received the nick name of BROM BONES,[7] by which he was universally known. He was famed for great knowledge and skill in horsemanship, being as dexterous on horse back as a Tartar.

---

[7] Anm. d. Hrsg. Ein Wortspiel, von *trombones*, Posaunen.

Bei diesem Unternehmen fand er jedoch größere Schwierigkeiten, als gewöhnlich vor Zeiten einem irrenden Ritter zufielen, der meist nur mit Riesen, Zauberern, feurigen Drachen und ähnlichen leicht besiegbaren Gegnern zu kämpfen und sich bloß durch eiserne und eherne Pforten, durch Diamantmauern den Weg zu dem Burgturm zu bahnen hatte, wo die Gebieterin seines Herzens gefangen saß; was er alles so leicht vollbrachte, wie ein Mann eine Pastete bis in die Mitte durchbohrt, worauf er, wie sich versteht, die Hand der holden Jungfrau erhielt. Ichabod hingegen mußte sich den Weg zum Herzen eines gefallsüchtigen liebelnden Landmädchens bahnen, wo er in einen Irrgang von Torheiten und Launen kam, die immer neue Schwierigkeiten und Hindernisse zeigten; er hatte es mit einem Heer furchtbarer Gegner von Fleisch und Blut aufzunehmen: den zahllosen ländlichen Verehrern, die jeden Zugang zu ihrem Herzen besetzten, mit einem wachsamen und unmutigen Auge einander bewachten, aber nichtsdestotrotz bereit waren, stets gemeinsame Sache gegen jeden neuen Mitbewerber zu machen.

Unter diesen Freiern war niemand so furchtbar, als ein ungeschlachter, lärmender, prahlerischer Gesell namens Abraham, oder – nach holländischer Abkürzung – Brom Van Brunt; der Held der Umgegend, von dessen Stärke und Kühnheit man sich viele Geschichten zu erzählen wußte. Er war breitschultrig und von starkem Knochenbau, mit kurzem, krausen schwarzen Haare, und einem schroffen, aber nicht unangenehmen Gesicht, dessen Ausdruck eine Mischung von Kurzweil und Übermut war. Seine Riesengestalt und große Stärke hatten zu dem Spottnamen Knochen-Brom Anlaß gegeben, worunter er allgemein bekannt war. Man rühmte seine ungemeine Kunst und Geschicklichkeit im Reiten, und in der Tat saß er zu Pferd wie ein Tatar.

He was foremost at all races and cock-fights: and with the ascendancy which bodily strength always acquires in rustic life, was the umpire in all disputes, setting his hat on one side, and giving his decisions with an air and tone that admitted of no gainsay or appeal. He was always ready for either a fight or a frolic; had more mischief than ill-will in his composition; and with all his overbearing roughness, there was a strong dash of waggish good humour at bottom. He had three or four boon companions of his own stamp, who regarded him as their model, and at the head of whom he scoured the country, attending every scene of feud or merriment for miles round. In cold weather he was distinguished by a fur cap, surmounted with a flaunting fox's tail; and when the folks at a country gathering descried this well-known crest at a distance, whisking about among a squad of hard riders, they always stood by for a squall. Sometimes his crew would be heard dashing along past the farm-houses at midnight, with whoop and halloo, like a troop of Don Cossacks: and the old dames, startled out of their sleep, would listen for a moment till the hurry-scurry had clattered by, and then exclaim, "Ay, there goes Brom Bones and his gang!" The neighbours looked upon him with a mixture of awe, admiration, and good-will; and when any mad-cap prank, or rustic brawl, occurred in the vicinity, always shook their heads, and warranted Brom Bones was at the bottom of it.

Bei jedem Wettrennen und Hahnenkampf war er an der Spitze, und bei der Überlegenheit, die Leibesstärke immer unter dem Landvolke gewinnt, wurde er in allen Streitigkeiten zum Schiedsrichter berufen, wobei er dann seinen Hut auf ein Ohr setzte und seine Entscheidungen mit einer Miene und einem Tone kundtat, wogegen weder Widerspruch, noch Berufung stattfand. Er war stets ebenso bereit zum Fechten, wie zu einem Spaße; mehr zu Possen als zu boshaften Streichen geneigt, und bei aller hochfahrenden Grobheit war doch ein starker Zug von mutwilliger guter Laune in seinem Wesen. Mit drei oder vier munteren Gesellen, die ihm im Verhalten glichen, durchstreifte er die Gegend, und war unfehlbar zur Stelle, wo es in meilenweitem Umkreis Streit oder Kurzweil gab. Bei kaltem Wetter trug er eine Pelzkappe mit einem herabhängenden Fuchsschwanz, und wenn die versammelten Landleute diesen wohlbekannten Helmbusch in der Ferne unter einem Haufen rascher Reiter flattern sahen, erwarteten sie immer eine Sturmböe. Zuweilen hörte man seine Rotte um Mitternacht mit lautem Geschrei, wie einen Schwarm Kosaken, vor den Wohnungen der Landleute vorüber fliegen, und wenn die alten Weiber, aus dem Schlafe aufgeschreckt, eine Weile gehorcht hatten, bis das Getöse vorüber war, riefen sie aus: „O das ist Knochen-Brom mit seiner Bande!" Die Nachbarn betrachteten ihn mit Furcht, Bewunderung und Wohlwollen zugleich, und wenn irgendein toller Streich oder eine Zänkerei in der Gegend vorfiel, schüttelten sie immer die Köpfe, und wetteten, Knochen-Brom hätte die Hand im Spiel.

This rantipole hero had for some time singled out the blooming Katrina for the object of his uncouth gallantries, and though his amorous toyings were something like the gentle caresses and endearments of a bear, yet it was whispered that she did not altogether discourage his hopes. Certain it is, his advances were signals for rival candidates to retire, who felt no inclination to cross a lion in his amours; insomuch, that when his horse was seen tied to Van Tassel's paling, on a Sunday night, a sure sign that his master was courting, or, as it is termed, "sparking," within, all other suitors passed by in despair, and carried the war into other quarters.

Such was the formidable rival with whom Ichabod Crane had to contend, and, considering all things, a stouter man than he would have shrunk from the competition, and a wiser man would have despaired. He had, however, a happy mixture of pliability and perseverance in his nature; he was in form and spirit like a supple jack—yielding, but tough; though he bent, he never broke; and though he bowed beneath the slightest pressure, yet, the moment it was away—jerk!—he was as erect, and carried his head as high as ever.

To have taken the field openly against his rival would have been madness; for he was not a man to be thwarted in his amours, any more than that stormy lover, Achilles. Ichabod, therefore, made his advances in a quiet and gently-insinuating manner. Under cover of his character of singing master, he made frequent visits at the farm-house; not that he had anything to apprehend from the meddlesome interference of parents, which is so often a stumbling-block in the path of lovers.

Dieser wilde Held hatte eine Zeitlang die blühende Katrina zum Gegenstand seiner ungeschliffenen Liebeswerbung ausersehen, und obgleich seine verliebten Tändeleien zuweilen den Schmeicheleien und Liebkosungen eines Bären glichen, so wurde doch gemunkelt, sie hätte seine Hoffnungen nicht ganz entmutigt. So viel ist gewiß, seine Bewerbungen waren für seine Nebenbuhler die Losung zum Rückzug, da niemand Lust hatte, einen Löwen bei seiner Brautwerbung zu stören, und wenn an einem Sonntagabend sein Pferd an Van Tassels Zaun gebunden war, ein Zeichen, daß der Reiter im Haus um die Holde warb, so gingen alle anderen Werber trostlos vorüber, um sich einen anderen Kampfplatz zu suchen.

Dies war der furchtbare Nebenbuhler, mit welchem Ichabod Crane zu kämpfen hatte, und wenn man alles bedachte, hätte ein rüstigerer Mann, als er es war, sich von der Bewerbung abschrecken lassen, und ein klügerer Mann wäre untröstlich gewesen. Es lag jedoch eine so glückliche Mischung von Geschmeidigkeit und Ausdauer in seinem Wesen, daß er in Gestalt und Geist wie ein guter Spazierstock war, nachgiebig, aber zäh; er bog sich, brach aber nie; und krümmte er sich auch unter dem leichtesten Drucke, so war jener doch kaum vorbei, ehe er so aufrecht stand und den Kopf so hoch trug, als zuvor.

Es wäre Wahnsinn gewesen, in offenen Kampf mit einem Nebenbuhler zu treten, der sich in seiner Liebe so wenig in die Quere kommen ließ, wie der stürmische Liebhaber Achilles. Ichabod machte seine Bewerbungen darum auf eine stille, freundlich einschmeichelnde Weise. Unter dem Deckmantel seines Singmeisterberufes machte er häufige Besuche auf dem Gute, wiewohl er gar nichts von der zudringlichen Einmischung der Angehörigen zu fürchten hatte, die so oft ein Stein des Anstoßes auf dem Wege der Liebenden ist.

Balt Van Tassel was an easy indulgent soul; he loved his daughter better even than his pipe, and like a reasonable man and an excellent father, let her have way in every thing. His notable little wife, too, had enough to do to attend to her house-keeping and manage the poultry; for, as she sagely observed, ducks and geese are foolish things, and must be looked after, but girls can take care of themselves. Thus while the busy dame bustled about the house, or plied her spinning wheel at one end of the piazza, honest Balt would sit smoking his evening pipe at the other, watching the achievements of a little wooden warrior, who, armed with a sword in each hand, was most valiantly fighting the wind on the pinnacle of the barn. In the meantime, Ichabod would carry on his suit with the daughter by the side of the spring under the great elm, or sauntering along in the twilight, that hour so favourable to the lover's eloquence.

I profess not to know how women's hearts are wooed and won. To me they have always been matters of riddle and admiration. Some seem to have but one vulnerable point, or door of access; while others have a thousand avenues, and may be captured in a thousand different ways. It is a great triumph of skill to gain the former, but a still greater proof of generalship to maintain possession of the latter, for a man must battle for his fortress at every door and window. He that wins a thousand common hearts, is therefore entitled to some renown; but he who keeps undisputed sway over the heart of a coquette, is indeed a hero.

Baltus Van Tassel war ein leutseliger, nachsichtiger Mann; er liebte seine Tochter noch mehr als selbst seine Pfeife, und ließ, als verständiger Mann und trefflicher Vater, ihr in allen Dingen ihren Willen. Seine sorgsame Hausfrau hatte alle Hände damit voll, ihr Hauswesen in Ordnung zu halten und ihr Federvieh zu warten; denn, wie sie weislich bemerkte, sind Enten und Gänse närrische Dinger und fordern Aufsicht, Mädchen aber können für sich selber sorgen. Während die geschäftige Hausfrau im Haus waltete, oder an dem einen Ende der Veranda ihr Spinnrad antrieb, saß der ehrliche Baltus mit seinem Abendpfeifchen am andern, und beobachtete die Leistungen eines kleinen hölzernen Kriegers, welcher, mit einem Schwert in jeder Hand, auf der Zinne der Scheune sehr tapfer gegen den Wind kämpfte. Ichabod hofierte unterdessen die Tochter am Quell unter der großen Ulme, oder schlenderte mit ihr in der Dämmerung umher, in jener Zeit, die der Beredsamkeit des Liebenden so günstig ist.

Ich gestehe, es ist mir unbekannt, wie man um Frauenherzen wirbt und sie gewinnt. Für mich sind sie stets Rätsel und Gegenstände der Bewunderung gewesen. Einige scheinen nur einen verwundbaren Punkt, nur einen Zugang zu haben, während es bei anderen tausend Wege gibt, und sie auf tausenderlei Art gewonnen werden können. Es ist ein großer Sieg der Geschicklichkeit, jene zu gewinnen, aber ein weit größerer Beweis von Feldherrnkunst, sich im Besitze der letzten zu behaupten, da der Inhaber der Festung an jedem Tor und Fenster kämpfen muß. Wer tausend gewöhnliche Herzen gewinnt, hat daher auf einigen Ruhm Anspruch, wer aber eine unbestrittene Herrschaft über das Herz eines gefallsüchtigen Mädchens behauptet, ist wahrhaft ein Held.

Certain it is, this was not the case with the redoubtable Brom Bones; and from the moment Ichabod Crane made his advances, the interests of the former evidently declined; his horse was no longer seen tied at the palings on Sunday nights, and a deadly feud gradually arose between him and the preceptor of Sleepy Hollow.

Brom, who had a degree of rough chivalry in his nature, would fain have carried matters to open warfare, and have settled their pretensions to the lady, according to the mode of those most concise and simple reasoners, the knights-errant of yore—by single combat; but Ichabod was too conscious of the superior might of his adversary to enter the lists against him; he had overheard the boast of Bones, that he would "double the schoolmaster up, and put him on a shelf;" and he was too wary to give him an opportunity. There was something extremely provoking in this obstinately pacific system; it left Brom no alternative but to draw upon the funds of rustic waggery in his disposition, and to play off boorish practical jokes upon his rival. Ichabod became the object of whimsical persecution to Bones, and his gang of rough riders.

Dies war sicherlich nicht der Fall bei dem furchtbaren Knochen-Brom, und von dem Augenblicke an, wo Ichabod Crane seine Bewerbungen begann, nahm Abrahams Ansehen sichtbar ab; sein Pferd wurde an Sonntagabenden nicht mehr am Zaun gesehen, und es entstand allmählich eine tödliche Feindschaft zwischen ihm und dem Schulmeister von Sleepy Hollow.

Brom, in dessen Wesen etwas von roher Ritterlichkeit lag, hätte die Sache gern im offenen Kampf ausgetragen, und ihre beiderseitigen Ansprüche auf die Jungfrau nach der Sitte jener sehr bündigen und einfachen Vernünftler, der fahrenden Ritter der Vorzeit, durch einen Zweikampf verhandelt; Ichabod aber kannte die überlegene Macht seines Widersachers zu gut, als daß er gegen ihn in die Schranken hätte treten mögen. Hatte doch Knochen-Brom sich gerühmt, er wollte den Schulmeister sehr unsanft betten, und dieser war zu vorsichtig, seinem Gegner dazu einen Anlaß zu geben. Brom war diese hartnäckige Friedensneigung höchst ärgerlich, und es blieb ihm nichts übrig, als seinem bäurischen Mutwillen Raum zu geben und seinen Nebenbuhler mit einigen derben Scherzen zu belästigen. Ichabod wurde nun der Gegenstand der eigensinnigen Verfolgung Knochen-Broms und seiner wilden Gesellen.

They harried his hitherto peaceful domains; smoked out his singing school, by stopping up the chimney; broke into the school house at night, in spite of its formidable fastenings of withe and window stakes, and turned everything topsy-turvy: so that the poor schoolmaster began to think all the witches in the country held their meetings there. But what was still more annoying, Brom took all opportunities of turning him into ridicule in presence of his mistress, and had a scoundrel dog whom he taught to whine in the most ludicrous manner, and introduced as a rival of Ichabod's, to instruct her in psalmody.

In this way matters went on for some time, without producing any material effect on the relative situations of the contending powers. On a fine autumnal afternoon, Ichabod, in pensive mood, sat enthroned on the lofty stool from whence he usually watched all the concerns of his little literary realm. In his hand he swayed a ferule, that sceptre of despotic power; the birch of justice reposed on three nails, behind the throne, a constant terror to evil doers; while on the desk before him might be seen sundry contraband articles and prohibited weapons, detected upon the persons of idle urchins; such as half-munched apples, popguns, whirligigs, fly-cages, and whole legions of rampant little paper game cocks. Apparently there had been some appalling act of justice recently inflicted, for his scholars were all busily intent upon their books, or slyly whispering behind them with one eye kept upon the master; and a kind of buzzing stillness reigned throughout the school-room.

Sie quälten des Schulmeisters zeither so friedsames Gebiet; trieben durch Verstopfung des Schornsteins den Rauch in seine Singschule, brachen zur Nachtzeit in seine Schulstube ein, trotz der wunderbaren Befestigungen mit Weidenruten und Pfählen an den Fenstern, und richteten ein solches Durcheinander an, daß der arme Schulmeister fast zu glauben begann, daß alle Hexen des Landes dort ihre Versammlungen abhielten; und was noch quälender war, Knochen-Brom ergriff jede Gelegenheit, ihn in Gegenwart der geliebten Katrina lächerlich zu machen, und hatte einem schelmischen Hund, der abgerichtet war, auf die spaßhafteste Art zu winseln, und sich als Ichabods Nebenbuhler einführte, um sie im Psalmsingen zu unterrichten.

Auf diese Art ging die Sache eine Zeitlang fort, ohne auf die jeweilige Lage der streitenden Parteien wesentlichen Einfluß zu haben. An einem schönen Herbstnachmittag saß Ichabod gedankenvoll auf dem hohen Stuhle, wo er gewöhnlich alle Angelegenheiten seines kleinen gelehrten Gebietes besorgte. Er schwang in der Hand eine Rute, das Zepter seiner Herrscherwillkür; das Birkenreis der Gerechtigkeit lag auf drei Nägeln hinter dem Thron, ein steter Schrecken der Übeltäter, während vor ihm auf dem Tische verschiedene, bei den kleinen Schelmen gefundene, unerlaubte Dinge und verbotene Waffen lagen, wie halb abgenagte Äpfel, Korkenbüchsen, Kreisel, Wunderdreher, und ganze Schwärme von papiernen Kampfhähnen. Wahrscheinlich war soeben ein abschreckender Akt der Gerechtigkeit ausgeübt worden, da jeder Schüler emsig auf seine Bücher sah, oder, ein Auge auf den Lehrer heftend, verstohlen mit seinem Hintermanne flüsterte, und es herrschte eine Art summende Stille in der Schulstube.

It was suddenly interrupted by the appearance of a negro in tow-cloth jacket and trowsers, a round crowned fragment of a hat, like the cap of Mercury, and mounted on the back of a ragged, wild, half-broken colt, which he managed with a rope by way of halter. He came clattering up to the school door with an invitation to Ichabod to attend a merry-making, or "quilting frolick," to be held that evening at Mynheer Van Tassel's; and having delivered his message with that air of importance, and effort at fine language, which a negro is apt to display on petty embassies of the kind, he dashed over the brook, and was seen scampering away up the hollow, full of the importance and hurry of his mission.

All was now bustle and hubbub in the late quiet school-room. The scholars were hurried through their lessons, without stopping at trifles; those who were nimble, skipped over half with impunity, and those who were tardy, had a smart application now and then in the rear, to quicken their speed, or help them over a tall word. Books were flung aside, without being put away on the shelves; inkstands were overturned; benches thrown down; and the whole school was turned loose an hour before the usual time; bursting forth like a legion of young imps, yelping and racketing about the green, in joy at their early emancipation.

The gallant Ichabod now spent at least an extra half hour at his toilet, brushing and furbishing up his best, and indeed only suit of rusty black, and arranging his looks by a bit of broken looking glass, that hung up in the school-house.

Plötzlich ward die Ruhe unterbrochen durch die Ankunft eines Negers in einem Leinenwams und Kniebundhosen und mit einem rundlichen Hutbruchstücke, einer Merkurkappe gleich, der auf einem zottigen, wilden, halb zugerittenen Pferd ritt, das er mit einem Strick anstelle einer Trense lenkte. Er kam vor die Türe des Schulhauses, mit der Einladung an Ichabod, an diesem Abend einer fröhlichen Zusammenkunft in Mynheer Van Tassels Haus beizuwohnen. Als er diesen Auftrag mit der wichtigen Miene und dem Streben nach schönen Worten, wodurch ein Neger bei solchen Botschaften sich auszuzeichnen sucht, ausgerichtet hatte, setzte er über den Bach, und eilte ins Tal, stolz auf die wichtige und eilige Mission.

Alles war nun in Aufstand und Unruhe im früher so ruhigen Schulhaus. Die Schüler wurden durch ihre Aufgaben gehetzt, ohne sich bei Kleinigkeiten aufzuhalten; die Hastigen kamen fast ohne Strafe weg, und die langsamen wurden von Zeit zu Zeit durch eine Schmerzzufügung zur Eile angetrieben, oder um ihnen über ein schweres Wort hinaus zu helfen. Die Bücher wurden auf die Seite geworfen, ohne sie auf die Simse zu stellen; Tintenfässer umgestoßen, Bänke umgeworfen, und eine Stunde vor der gewöhnlichen Zeit die Schüler entlassen, die wie ein Schwarm junger Bienen hervorbrachen, schreiend und lärmend über ihre frühe Befreiung.

Der verliebte Ichabod widmete wenigstens eine halbe Stunde mehr seinem Putze, bürstete und putzte seinen besten, und in der Tat seinen einzigen, schon abgenutzten schwarzen Anzug, und machte seine Haare vor einer Spiegelscherbe zurecht, die in der Schulstube hing.

That he might make his appearance before his mistress in the true style of a cavalier, he borrowed a horse from the farmer with whom he was domiciliated, a choleric old Dutchman, of the name of Hans Van Ripper, and thus gallantly mounted, issued forth like a knight-errant in quest of adventures. But it, is meet I should, in the true spirit of romantic story, give some account of the looks and equipments of my hero and his steed. The animal he bestrode was a broken-down plough horse, that had outlived almost every thing but his viciousness. He was gaunt and shagged, with a ewe neck and a head like a hammer; his rusty mane and tail were tangled and knotted with burs; one eye had lost its pupil, and was glaring and spectral; but the other had the gleam of a genuine devil in it. Still he must have had fire and mettle in his day, if we may judge from his name, which was Gunpowder. He had, in fact, been a favourite steed of his master's, the choleric Van Ripper, who was a furious rider, and had infused, very probably, some of his own spirit into the animal; for, old and broken-down as he looked, there was more lurking deviltry in him than in any young filly in the country.

Ichabod was a suitable figure for such a steed. He rode with short stirrups, which brought his knees nearly up to the pommel of the saddle: his sharp elbows stuck out like grasshoppers'; he carried his whip perpendicularly in his hand, like a sceptre, and as the horse jogged on, the motion of his arms was not unlike the flapping of a pair of wings.

Um vor seiner Geliebten als wahrer Kavalier zu erscheinen, borgte er sich ein Pferd von dem Bauern, bei welchem er wohnte, einem zähzornigen alten Holländer namens Hans Van Ripper, und derart wacker beritten, brach er auf, wie ein fahrender Ritter, Abenteuer zu suchen. Es ziemt sich jedoch, daß ich im wahren Geiste der romantischen Geschichte etwas über das Aussehen und die Ausstattung meines Helden und seines Rosses berichte. Sein Pferd war ein abgenutzter Ackergaul, der fast alles überlebt hatte, bis auf seine Bösartigkeit. Es war dürr und zottig, hatte einen Hals wie ein Schaf und einen Kopf wie ein Hammer; seine Mähne und sein Schweif, von rostfarbigem Ansehen, waren verwirrt und mit Kletten besetzt; das eine Auge hatte die Sehkraft verloren und glänzte gespenstisch, das andere aber blitzte wie vom Teufel belebt. Zu seiner Zeit mochte es jedoch feurig und mutig genug gewesen sein, wie sein Name, *Gunpowder*[8], anzudeuten schien. Es war einst der Liebling seines Herrn, des cholerischen Van Ripper, gewesen, der ein wilder Reiter war, und ohne Zweifel dem Tiere etwas von seinem Geiste mitgeteilt hatte, denn so alt und abgenutzt es aussah, hatte es doch ein teuflischeres Wesen als irgendein junges Füllen im Lande.

Ichabods Gestalt paßte zu seinem Reittier. Er ritt mit kurzen Steigbügeln, die seine Knie fast bis zum Sattelknauf hoben: seine spitzen Ellbogen ragten wie Heuschreckenbeine hervor; er hielt seine Peitsche senkrecht in der Hand, wie ein Zepter, und als sein Pferd sich fortbewegte, bewegten sich seine Arme wie Flügel auf und ab.

---

[8] Schießpulver.

A small wool hat rested on the top of his nose, for so his scanty strip of forehead might be called; and the skirts of his black coat fluttered out almost to the horse's tail. Such was the appearance of Ichabod and his steed, as they shambled out of the gate of Hans Van Ripper, and it was altogether such an apparition as is seldom to be met with in broad daylight.

It was, as I have said, a fine autumnal day; the sky was clear and serene, and nature wore that rich and golden livery which we always associate with the idea of abundance. The forests had put on their sober brown and yellow, while some trees of the tenderer kind had been nipped by the frosts into brilliant dyes of orange, purple, and scarlet. Streaming files of wild ducks began to make their appearance high in the air; the bark of the squirrel might be heard from the groves of beech and hickory nuts, and the pensive whistle of the quail at intervals from the neighbouring stubble field.

The small birds were taking their farewell banquets. In the fulness of their revelry, they fluttered, chirping and frolicking, from bush to bush, and tree to tree, capricious from the very profusion and variety around them.

Ein kleiner Filzhut ruhte auf der Nasenwurzel, wie man den knappen Streif von einer Stirne wohl nennen konnte, und die Schöße seines schwarzen Rockes flatterten beinahe bis zum Schweif des Pferdes hinab. So sah man Ichabod und sein Roß, als sie sperrbeinig aus Van Rippers Tore hervorschritten, und es war wohl eine Erscheinung, wie man sie selten bei hellem Tageslichte erblickt.

Es war, wie ich erwähnte, ein schöner Herbsttag. Der Himmel war klar und heiter, und die Natur trug das kostbare, goldene Gewand, das wir immer mit dem Gedanken an Überfluß verbinden. Die Wälder hatten ihr bescheidenes Braun und Gelb angelegt, aber einige zartere Bäume, vom Frost angegriffen, wiesen leuchtende Farben in Orange, Purpur und Scharlach auf. Langgezogene Schwärme wilder Enten ließen sich in der Luft sehen; der Ruf des Eichhörnchens tönte laut in den Wäldchen von Buchen und Hickorynußbäumen[9] und das sinnende Pfeifen der Wachtel zuweilen im nahen Stoppelfelde.

Die kleineren Vögel nahmen ihr Abschiedsmahl. In ihrem Jubel flatterten, zirpten und taumelten sie von Busch zu Busch, von Baum zu Baum, und waren wählerisch, gerade weil sie so viel Überfluß und Abwechslung rings umher fanden.

---

[9] Der weiße amerikanische Walnußbaum – Juglans alba.

There was the honest cock-robin, the favourite game of stripling sportsmen, with its loud querulous note; and the twittering blackbirds flying in sable clouds; and the golden-winged woodpecker, with his crimson crest, his broad black gorget, and splendid plumage; and the cedar bird, with its red tipt wings and yellow tipt tail, and its little monteiro cap of feathers; and the blue jay, that noisy coxcomb, in his gay light blue coat and white under clothes; screaming and chattering, nodding and bobbing and bowing, and pretending to be on good terms with every songster of the grove.

As Ichabod jogged slowly on his way, his eye, ever open to every symptom of culinary abundance, ranged with delight over the treasures of jolly autumn. On all sides he beheld vast store of apples; some hanging in oppressive opulence on the trees; some gathered into baskets and barrels for the market; others heaped up in rich piles for the cider-press. Farther on he beheld great fields of Indian corn, with its golden ears peeping from their leafy coverts, and holding out the promise of cakes and hasty pudding; and the yellow pumpkins lying beneath them, turning up their fair round bellies to the sun, and giving ample prospects of the most luxurious of pies; and anon he passed the fragrant buckwheat fields, breathing the odour of the bee-hive, and as he beheld them, soft anticipations stole over his mind of dainty slap jacks, well buttered, and garnished with honey or treacle, by the delicate little dimpled hand of Katrina Van Tassel.

Thus feeding his mind with many sweet thoughts and "sugared suppositions," he journeyed along the sides of a range of hills which look out upon some of the goodliest scenes of the mighty Hudson.

Da war das ehrliche Rotkehlchen, welchem Knaben so gern nachstellen, mit seinem lauten Gesange; die zwitschernden Amseln, in ganzen Schwärmen fliegend, der goldbeschwingte Specht mit seinem roten Helmbusch, seinem breiten schwarzen Halsband, und glänzenden Gefieder; der Zedernvogel mit rot betupften Flügeln und gelb betupftem Schwanze, und seiner Federhaube, und der Blauhäher, der lärmende Geck mit seinem hellblauen Röckchen und weißen Unterkleidern, alle schreiend und schwatzend, nickend und neckend und neigend, und alle schienen in gutem Einvernehmen mit jedem Waldsänger stehen zu wollen.

Als Ichabod langsam seinen Weg entlang trabte, ließ er seinen Blick, der stets für alle Art von kostbaren Überflusse offen war, mit Behagen über die Schätze des wonnigen Herbstes streifen. Zu allen Seiten sah er unermeßliche Vorräte von Äpfeln; einige noch auf den schwer beladenen Bäumen, andere in Körben und Fässern für den Markt gesammelt, andere für die Apfelweinpresse zu großen Haufen aufgetürmt. Weiter in der Ferne sah er große Maisfelder, deren goldene Kolben aus der Blatthülle hervor blickten und Küchlein und Pudding versprachen; unter ihnen lagen die gelben Kürbisse, die ihre glatten runden Bäuche der Sonne zuwendeten und die köstlichsten Pasteten verhießen. Hier und da sah er Buchweizenfelder, die wie ein Bienenkorb dufteten, und bei diesem Anblick beschlich ihn eine süße Ahnung von köstlichen Pfannkuchen, mit Butter bestrichen, und mit Honig oder Sirup beträufelt von Katrinas zarter weiblichen Hand.

So fütterte er seinen Geist mit süßen Gedanken und „gezuckerten Hoffnungen", während er längs einer Hügelreihe ritt, die auf einige der reizendsten Landschaften am Ufer des mächtigen Hudson hinab schaute.

The sun gradually wheeled his broad disk down into the west. The wide bosom of the Tappaan Zee lay motionless and glassy, excepting that here and there a gentle undulation waved and prolonged the blue shadow of the distant mountain. A few amber clouds floated in the sky, without a breath of air to move them. The horizon was of a fine golden tint, changing gradually into a pure apple green, and from that into the deep blue of the mid-heaven. A slanting ray lingered on the woody crests of the precipices that overhung some parts of the river, giving greater depth to the dark grey and purple of her rocky sides. A sloop was loitering in the distance, dropping slowly down with the tide, her sail hanging uselessly against the mast; and as the reflection of the sky gleamed along the still water, it seemed as if the vessel was suspended in the air.

It was toward evening that Ichabod arrived at the castle of the Heer Van Tassel, which he found thronged with the pride and flower of the adjacent country. Old farmers, a spare leathern-faced race, in homespun coats and breeches, blue stockings, huge shoes and magnificent pewter buckles. Their brisk, withered, little dames in close crimped caps, long waisted short gowns, homespun petticoats, with scissors and pincushions, and gay calico pockets, hanging on the outside. Buxom lasses, almost as antiquated as their mothers, excepting where a straw hat, a fineriband, or perhaps a white frock, gave symptoms of city innovations.

Die Sonne schob ihre große Scheibe allmählich gen Westen. Der weite Busen des Tappaan-Zee lag wie ein glatter Spiegel, nur daß hier und da ein leiser Wellenschlag den blauen Schatten des fernen Gebirges bewegte und verlängerte. Einige bernsteinfarbene Wölkchen trieben am Himmel, ohne daß ein Lufthauch sie bewegt hätte. Allmählich verwandelte sich die schöne Goldfarbe des Himmelsrandes in ein reines Apfelgrün und verschwamm dann in das dunkle Blau der Himmelsmitte. Ein schräger Sonnenstrahl verweilte auf den waldigen Häuptern der steilen Höhen, welche an einigen Stellen über den Strom herabhingen und verlieh dem düsteren Grau und Purpur ihrer felsigen Seiten einen tieferen Farbton. Eine Schaluppe zögerte in der Ferne, langsam mit der Flut hinab fahrend, mit unnütz herabhängendem Segel, und da der Widerschein des Himmels auf dem stillen Wasser glänzte, schien das Fahrzeug wie in der Luft zu hängen.

Der Abend brach an, als Ichabod in Van Tassels Schloß ankam, wo er den Stolz und die Pracht der Nachbarschaft versammelt fand. Alte Bauern, ein abgelebtes Geschlecht, mit ledrigen Gesichtern, in hausgemachten Röcken und Beinkleidern, blauen Strümpfen und ungeheuren Schuhen mit prächtigen zinnernen Schnallen. Ihre munteren verwitterten Hausfrauen mit eng gefältelten Hauben, langen taillierten Kleidern, selbst gewebten Röcken, worauf Schere und Nadelkissen nebst Taschen von buntem Kaliko hingen. Dralle Mädchen, beinahe so veraltet gekleidet wie ihre Mütter, ausgenommen, wo ein Strohhut, ein schönes Band oder vielleicht ein weißes Kleid städtische Neuerung verrieten.

The sons in short square-skirted coats with rows of stupendous brass buttons, and their hair generally queued in the fashion of the times, especially if they could procure an eel-skin for the purpose, it being esteemed, throughout the country, as a potent nourisher and strengthener of the hair.

Brom Bones, however, was the hero of the scene, having come to the gathering on his favourite steed Daredevil, a creature, like himself, full of mettle and mischief, and which no one but himself could manage. He was, in fact, noted for preferring vicious animals, given to all kinds of tricks which kept the rider in constant risk of his neck, for he held a tractable well-broken horse as unworthy of a lad of spirit.

Fain would I pause to dwell upon the world of charms that burst upon the enraptured gaze of my hero, as he entered the state parlour of Van Tassel's mansion. Not those of the bevy of buxom lasses, with their luxurious display of red and white; but the ample charms of a genuine Dutch country tea-table, in the sumptuous time of autumn.

Such heaped up platters of cakes of various and almost indescribable kinds, known only to experienced Dutch housewives! There was the doughty dough-nut, the tenderer olykoek, and the crisp and crumbling cruller; sweet cakes and short cakes, ginger cakes and honey cakes, and the whole family of cakes.

Die Söhne in kurzen breitschößigen Röcken, mit ungeheuren messingenen Knöpfen besetzt, und das Haar nach damaliger Sitte zu einem Zopf gebunden, besonders wenn sie sich dazu eine Aalhaut hatten verschaffen können, die man im ganzen Lande für ein den Haarwuchs kräftig förderndes Mittel hielt.

Knochen-Brom aber war der Held des Festes. Er war auf seinem Lieblingspferde namens *Daredevil*[10] gekommen, einem Tier, das, wie er selber, voll Kühnheit und Schabernack war, und von ihm allein sich bändigen ließ. Es war bekannt, daß er bösartige Pferde vorzog, die durch ihre Tücke den Reiter stets halsbrechenden Gefahren aussetzen, und ein lenksames, gut zugerittenes Tier hielt er eines draufgängerischen Burschen für unwürdig.

Gern wollte ich die Reize schildern, die dem entzückten Blicke meines Helden begegneten, als er in Van Tassels prachtvolles Haus trat; nicht die Reize einer Schar draller Dirnen, die ihre üppige Fülle in Rot und Weiß zur Schau stellten; sondern wegen des lockenden Überflusses eines echt holländischen Teetisches in der Fülle der Herbstzeit.

Solche aufgehäuften Platten mit verschiedenen und fast unbeschreiblichen Arten von Kuchen, die nur erfahrenen holländischen Hausfrauen bekannt sind! Da waren stattliche Windbeutel, zartere Ölkuchen, mürbe bröckelndes Schmalzgebackenes, süße Kuchen und Teegebäck, Ingwerkuchen und Honigkuchen, und die ganze Kuchensippschaft.

[10] *Trotzteufel.*

And then there were apple pies and peach pies and pumpkin pies; besides slices of ham and smoked beef; and moreover delectable dishes of preserved plums, and peaches, and pears, and quinces; not to mention broiled shad and roasted chickens; together with bowls of milk and cream, all mingled higgledy-piggledy, pretty much as I have enumerated them, with the motherly tea pot sending up its clouds of vapour from the midst —Heaven bless the mark! I want breath and time to discuss this banquet as it deserves, and am too eager to get on with my story. Happily, Ichabod Crane was not in so great a hurry as his historian, but did ample justice to every dainty.

He was a kind and thankful toad, whose heart dilated in proportion as his skin was filled with good cheer; and whose spirits rose with eating as some men's do with drink. He could not help, too, rolling his large eyes round him as he ate, and chuckling with the possibility that he might one day be lord of all this scene of almost unimaginable luxury and splendour. Then, he thought, how soon he'd turn his back upon the old school-house; snap his fingers in the face of Hans Van Ripper, and every other niggardly patron, and kick any itinerant pedagogue out of doors that should dare to call him comrade!

Old Baltus Van Tassel moved about among his guests with a face dilated with content and good humour, round and jolly as the harvest moon.

Auch fehlten nicht Pasteten von Äpfeln, von Pfirsichen und Kürbissen; Scheiben von Schinken und geräuchertem Rindfleisch, köstliche Gerichte von eingemachten Pflaumen, Pfirsichen, Birnen und Quitten; nicht zu erwähnen gesottene Heringe und gebratene Hähnchen, mit Näpfen voll Milch und Rahm, alles untereinander wie Kraut und Rüben, oder beinahe wie ich's aufgezählt habe, samt der hausmütterlichen Teekanne, die mitten auf dem Tisch ihre Dampfwolken aufsteigen ließ. Lieber Himmel! es fehlt mir an Atem und Zeit, das Gastmahl nach Verdienst zu beschreiben, so eilig bin ich, mit meiner Geschichte weiter zu kommen. Ichabod aber war zum Glück nicht so sehr in Eile wie sein Geschichtschreiber, und ließ jedem Leckerbissen volles Recht widerfahren.

Er war eine gutmütige und nicht undankbare Kröte; sein Herz wurde weiter, je mehr er sich mit guter Leibesnahrung füllte, und wie bei einigen Menschen das Trinken, so hob bei ihm das Essen die Laune. Er konnte sich auch nicht enthalten, beim Essen seine großen Augen umher gleiten zu lassen, und sich heimlich der Möglichkeit zu freuen, daß all diese fast unvorstellbare Fülle und Herrlichkeit einst sein werden sollte. Dann dachte er daran, wie schnell er seinem alten Schulhaus den Rücken zuwenden wollte; wie er Hans Van Ripper und jedem andern knauserigen Gönner ein Schnippchen schlagen, und jeden wandernden Schulmeister, der ihn Kamerad nennen wollte, aus der Türe werfen wollte!

Der alte Baltus Van Tassel bewegte sich unter seinen Gästen, mit einem Gesicht, das Zufriedenheit und gute Laune so rund und fröhlich wie den Herbstmond machten.

His hospitable attentions were brief, but expressive, being confined to a shake of the hand, a slap on the shoulder, a loud laugh, and a pressing invita tion to "fall to, and help themselves."

And now the sound of the music from the common room, or hall, summoned to the dance. The musician was an old grey-headed negro, who had been the itinerant orchestra of the neighbourhood for more than half a century. His instrument was as old and battered as himself. The greater part of the time he scraped away on two or three strings, accompanying every movement of the bow with a motion of the head; bowing almost to the ground, and stamping with his foot whenever a fresh couple were to start.

Ichabod prided himself upon his dancing as much as upon his vocal powers. Not a limb, not a fibre about him was idle, and to have seen his loosely hung frame in full motion, and clattering about the room, you would have thought Saint Vitus himself, that blessed patron of the dance, was figuring before you in person. He was the admi- ration of all the negroes; who, having gathered, of all ages and sizes, from the farm and the neighbourhood, stood forming a pyramid of shining black faces at every door and window; gazing with delight at the scene; rolling their white eyeballs, and showing grinning rows of ivory from ear to ear. How could the flogger of urchins be otherwise than animated and joyous? the lady of his heart was his partner in the dance, and smiled graciously in reply to all his amorous oglings; while Brom Bones, sorely smitten with love and jealousy, sat brooding by himself in one corner.

When the dance was at an end, Ichabod was attracted to a knot of the sager folks, who, with old Van Tassel, sat smoking at one end of the piazza, gossiping over former times, and drawling out long stories about the war.

Seine gastfreundlichen Aufmerksamkeiten waren nicht umständlich, aber ausdruckvoll, und beschränkten sich auf einen Händedruck, einen Schlag auf die Schulter, ein lautes Auflachen und eine dringende Einladung, „zuzulangen und sich zu bedienen".

Die Musik rief nun zum Tanze. Der Spielmann war ein alter grauköpfiger Neger, der seit mehr als fünfzig Jahren das wandernde Orchester des Umlandes gewesen war. Sein Instrument war so alt und abgenutzt wie er selber. Den größten Teil der Zeit kratzte er auf zwei, oder drei Saiten, begleitete jeden Bogenstrich mit einer Bewegung des Kopfes, bückte sich fast bis auf die Erde, und stampfte mit dem Fuße, so oft ein neues Paar anfangen mußte.

Ichabod bildete sich so viel auf sein Tanzen ein wie auf seine Stimme. Nicht ein Glied, nicht eine Fiber an ihm war müßig, und sah man seine dürre Gestalt in voller Bewegung im Zimmer umher schlottern, so glaubte man Sankt Veit, den Schutzheiligen des Tanzes, höchstpersönlich vor sich zu sehen. Er ward bewundert von allen Negern, welche zahlreich, Alt und Jung, vom Gute und aus der Nachbarschaft herbeigekommen waren, und nun an jeder Tür und jedem Fenster eine Pyramide von glänzenden schwarzen Gesichtern bildeten, mit Entzücken dem Schauspiel zusahen, ihre weißen Augäpfel rollten und grinsende Elfenbeinreihen von einem Ohre zum andern sehen ließen. Wie hätte der Knabenpeitscher anders als lebendig und fröhlich sein können? Die Dame seines Herzens tanzte ja mit ihm, und erwiderte sein zärtliches Liebäugeln mit holdseligem Lächeln, während Knochen-Brom, von Liebe und Eifersucht heftig bewegt, vor sich hin brütend in einer Ecke saß.

Als der Tanz zu Ende war, zog es Ichabod zu dem Häuflein weiser Leute, die mit dem alten Van Tassel am Ende der Veranda eine Pfeife rauchten, von alten Zeiten schwatzten und lange Geschichten vom Krieg erzählten.

This neighbourhood, at the time of which I am speaking, was one of those highly favoured places which abound with chronicle and great men. The British and American line had run near it during the war; it had, therefore, been the scene of marauding, and infested with refugees, cowboys, and all kinds of border chivalry. Just sufficient time had elapsed to enable each story teller to dress up his tale with a little becoming fiction, and, in the indistinctness of his recollection, to make himself the hero of every exploit.

There was the story of Doffue Martling, a large blue-bearded Dutchman, who had nearly taken a British frigate with an old iron nine-pounder from a mud breastwork, only that his gun burst at the sixth discharge. And there was an old gentleman, who shall be nameless, being too rich a mynheer to be lightly mentioned, who, in the battle of Whiteplains, being an excellent master of defence, parried a musketball with a small sword, insomuch that he absolutely felt it whiz round the blade, and glance off at the hilt: in proof of which, he was ready at any time to show the sword, with the hilt a little bent. There were several more who had been equally great in the field, not one of whom but was persuaded that he had a considerable hand in bringing the war to a happy termination.

But all these were nothing to the tales of ghosts and apparitions that succeeded.

Diese Gegend war um die Zeit, wovon ich rede, einer der hoch begünstigten Orte, die reich an Sagen und großen Männern waren. Die britischen und amerikanischen Kriegsvölker hatten sich in der Nähe geschlagen, und dieser Bezirk war daher der Schauplatz von Räubereien gewesen, und von Flüchtlingen, von Cowboys und von Grenzrittertum aller Art heimgesucht worden. Es war gerade genug Zeit verflossen, daß jeder Erzähler sein Geschichtchen mit gebührender Dichtung ausschmücken und bei der Unbestimmtheit seiner Erinnerung sich selber zum Helden aller Taten machen konnte.

So erzählte man von Doffue Martling, einem dicken blaubärtigen Holländer, der beinahe eine englische Fregatte mit einem alten eisernen Neunpfünder von einer schlammigen Feldschanze aus genommen hätte, wenn nicht das Stück beim sechsten Schusse gesprungen wäre. Und da gab es einen alten Herrn, dessen Namen ich nicht nennen will, weil er ein zu reicher Mynheer ist, als daß er leichtfertig erwähnt werden dürfte, und der, als ein Meister in der Verteidigung, in der Schlacht bei White Plains eine Flintenkugel mit seinem Degen so gut abgewehrt hatte, daß sie an der Klinge hinpfiff und am Griff abstreifte, wie er denn zu jeder Zeit bereit war, den Degen mit dem etwas verbogenen Griff zu zeigen. Es gab noch mehre andere, die ebenso viele Großtaten im Felde vollbracht hatten, und es gab keinen unter ihnen, der nicht überzeugt gewesen wäre, daß er maßgeblich dazu beigetragen hätte, den Krieg zu einem glücklichen Ende zu bringen.

Doch all dies war nichts gegen die Geschichten von Geistern und Erscheinungen, die darauf folgten.

The neighbourhood is rich in legendary treasures of the kind. Local tales and superstitions thrive best in these sheltered long settled retreats; but are trampled under foot by the shifting throng that forms the population of most of our country places. Besides there is no encouragement for ghosts in most of our villages, for they have scarce had time to take their first nap, and turn themselves in their graves, before their surviving friends have travelled away from the neighbourhood; so that when they turn out at night to walk their rounds, they have no acquaintance left to call upon. This is perhaps the reason why we so seldom hear of ghosts except in our long-established Dutch communities.

The immediate cause, however, of the prevalence of supernatural stories in these parts, was doubtless owing to the vicinity of Sleepy Hollow. There was a contagion in the very air that blew from that haunted region; it breathed forth an atmosphere of dreams and fancies infecting all the land. Several of the Sleepy Hollow people were present at Van Tassel's, and, as usual, were doling out their wild and wonderful legends. Many dismal tales were told about funeral trains, and mournful cries and wailings heard and seen about the great tree where the unfortunate Major André was taken, and which stood in the neighbourhood. Some mention was made also of the woman in white, that haunted the dark glen at Raven Rock, and was often heard to shriek on winter nights before a storm, having perished there in the snow.

Die Gegend ist reich an Märchenschätzen dieser Art; örtliche Sagen und abergläubische Meinungen gedeihen am besten in diesen abgeschirmten, abgeschiedenen alten Ansiedlungen, werden aber durch das bewegliche Gedränge, das die Volksmenge unter den Bewohnern unserer meisten ländlichen Ansiedlungen herbeiführt, zertreten. In der Mehrzahl unsrer Dörfer gibt es auch keine Aufmunterung für Gespenster, da sie kaum Zeit gehabt hatten, ihr erstes Nickerchen zu halten und sich im Grabe umzuwenden, als schon ihre überlebenden Freunde aus der Gegend weggezogen waren, weshalb sie denn auf ihren nächtlichen Gängen keine Bekannten finden, welchen sie einen Besuch abstatten könnten. Dies ist vielleicht die Ursache, warum wir so selten von Geistern hören, außer in unseren alten holländischen Ansiedlungen.

Die nächste Ursache der Verbreitung von Gespenstergeschichten in dieser Gegend lag jedoch zweifellos an der Nähe zu Sleepy Hollow. Selbst die Luft, die aus jenem gespenstischen Gebiete wehte, enthielt etwas Ansteckendes, das Träume und Einbildungen in der ganzen Gegend verbreitete. Es waren mehrere Leute aus Sleepy Hollow in Van Tassels Haus und gaben, wie gewöhnlich, ihre tollen Wundergeschichten zum Besten. Man hörte viele furchtbare Geschichten von Leichenzügen, und von traurigem Geschrei und Wehklagen bei dem großen Baume in der Nachbarschaft, wo der unglückliche Major André gefangen worden war. Auch wurde der weißen Frau gedacht, die im finsteren Tale bei *Raven Rock*[II] spukte, und deren Geschrei oft in Winternächten vor einem Sturme gehört wurde, da sie hier einst im Schnee umgekommen war.

[II] *Rabenfels.*

The chief part of the stories, however, turned upon the favourite spectre of Sleepy Hollow, the headless horseman, who had been heard several times of late, patrolling the country; and, it was said, tethered his horse nightly among the graves in the churchyard.

The sequestered situation of this church seems always to have made it a favourite haunt of troubled spirits. It stands on a knoll, surrounded by locust trees and lofty elms, from among which its decent, whitewashed walls shine modestly forth, like Christian purity, beaming through the shades of retirement. A gentle slope descends from it to a silver sheet of water, bordered by high trees, between which, peeps may be caught at the blue hills of the Hudson. To look upon its grass grown yard, where the sunbeams seem to sleep so quietly, one would think that there at least the dead might rest in peace. On one side of the church extends a wide woody dell, along which raves a large brook among broken rocks and trunks of fallen trees. Over a deep black part of the stream, not far from the church, was formerly thrown a wooden bridge; the road that led to it, and the bridge itself, were thickly shaded by overhanging trees, which cast a gloom about it, even in the day-time; but occasioned a fearful darkness at night. Such was one of the favourite haunts of the headless horseman, and the place where he was most frequently encountered.

Die meisten Geschichten aber betrafen das Lieblings-gespenst von Sleepy Hollow, den kopflosen Reiter, der in letzter Zeit häufig gesehen wurde, wie er seine Streifzüge machte, und sein Pferd unter den Gräbern auf dem Kirchhofe angebunden haben sollte.

Die Kirche scheint wegen ihrer Abgelegenheit zu allen Zeiten ein Lieblingsplatz unruhiger Geister gewesen zu sein. Sie liegt auf einer Anhöhe, von Robinien und hohen Ulmen umgeben, aus welchen ihre weißen Mauern be-scheiden hervorblicken, wie christliche Sittenreinheit aus den Schatten der Abgeschiedenheit. Ein sanfter Abhang senkt sich zu einem silbernen Wasserspiegel, von hohen Bäumen umgeben, zwischen welchen die blauen Hudson-Berge hervorblicken. Betrachtete man den grasbewachsenen Kirchhof, wo die Sonnenstrahlen so ruhig zu schlafen schienen, so hätte man denken sollen, daß dort zumindest die Toten in Frieden ruhen könnten. Auf der einen Seite der Kirche verläuft ein breites bewaldetes Tal, durch welches ein großer Bach zwischen Felsbrocken und umgestürzten Baumstämmen wild hinabrauscht. Über eine tiefe dunkle Stelle des Waldbaches, nicht weit von der Kirche, ging vor Zeiten eine hölzerne Brücke, und der dahin führende Pfad, sowie die Brücke selbst, waren dicht beschattet von über-hängenden Bäumen, die selbst bei Tage Düsternis verbrei-teten, aber bei Nacht eine furchtbare Finsternis bewirkten. Dies war einer der Lieblingsorte des kopflosen Reiters, und der Ort, wo man ihn am häufigsten sah.

The tale was told of old Brouwer, a most heretical disbeliever in ghosts, how he met the horseman returning from his foray into Sleepy Hollow, and was obliged to get up behind him; how they galloped over bush and brake, over hill and swamp, until they reached the bridge; when the horseman suddenly turned into a skeleton, threw old Brouwer into the brook, and sprang away over the tree-tops with a clap of thunder.

This story was immediately matched by a thrice marvellous adventure of Brom Bones, who made light of the Galloping Hessian as an arrant jockey. He affirmed, that on returning one night from the neighbouring village of Sing-Sing, he had been overtaken by this midnight trooper; that he had offered to race with him for a bowl of punch, and should have won it too, for Daredevil beat the goblin horse all hollow, but just as they came to the church bridge, the Hessian bolted, and vanished in a flash of fire.

All these tales, told in that drowsy under-tone with which men talk in the dark, the countenances of the listeners only now and then receiving a casual gleam from the glare of a pipe, sunk deep in the mind of Ichabod. He repaid them in kind with large extracts from his invaluable author, Cotton Mather, and added many marvellous events that had taken place in his native state of Connecticut, and fearful sights which he had seen in his nightly walks about Sleepy Hollow.

Man erzählte, wie der alte Brouwer, bekannt durch seinen ketzerischen Unglauben an Geister, auf den Reiter gestoßen, als dieser von seinem Streifzuge nach Sleepy Hollow zurückkehrte, und gezwungen gewesen war, sich hinter ihn zu setzen; wie sie über Busch und Gestrüpp, über Hügel und Sumpf gesprengt waren, bis sie die Brücke erreicht hatten, wo der Reiter sich plötzlich in ein Gerippe verwandelte, den alten Mann in den Bach warf, und mit einem Donnerschlag über die Wipfel der Bäume davonsprang.

Dieser Erzählung folgte ein dreimal so wunderbares Abenteuer von Knochen-Brom, der von dem galoppierenden Hessen so geringschätzig wie von einem gemeinen Wettreiter sprach. Er war einst, wie er behauptete, bei der Rückkehr aus dem benachbarten Dorfe Sing-Sing, von dem nächtlichen Reitersmann eingeholt worden, worauf er ihm denn einen Wettritt um eine Schale Punsch vorgeschlagen hatte, und er würde auch gewonnen haben, da das Gespensterpferd mit Daredevil nicht mithalten konnte, aber als sie an die Kirchenbrücke kamen, hielt der Hesse und verschwand in einem Feuerblitz.

Alle diese Geschichten, in dem dumpfen Tone erzählt, womit Männer im Finstern zu sprechen pflegen, während die Gesichter der Zuhörer nur zuweilen von dem Glutschein einer Tabakspfeife beleuchtet wurden, machten einen tiefen Eindruck auf Ichabod. Er gab dafür zur Vergeltung reichliche Auszüge aus seinem unschätzbaren Cotton Mather zum Besten, und erzählte viele wunderbare Begebenheiten, die sich in seiner Heimat Connecticut zugetragen hatten, und furchtbare Geschichten, Erscheinungen, die er auf seinen nächtlichen Wanderungen in der Gegend von Sleepy Hollow gesehen habe.

The revel now gradually broke up. The old farmers gathered together their families in their waggons, and were heard for some time rattling along the hollow roads, and over the distant hills. Some of the damsels mounted on pillions behind their favourite swains, and their light-hearted laughter, mingling with the clatter of hoofs, echoed along the silent woodlands, sounding fainter and fainter until they gradually died away—and the late scene of noise and frolick was all silent and deserted. Ichabod only lingered behind, according to the custom of country lovers, to have a tête-à-tête with the heiress; fully convinced that he was now on the high road to success.

What passed at this interview I will not pretend to say, for in fact I do not know. Something, however, I fear me, must have gone wrong, for he certainly sallied forth, after no very great interval, with an air quite desolate and chopfallen–Oh these women! these women! Could that girl have been playing off any of her coquettish tricks?—Was her encouragement of the poor pedagogue all a mere sham to secure her conquest of his rival?—Heaven only knows, not I'—Let it suffice to say, Ichabod stole forth with the air of one who had been sacking a hen-roost, rather than a fair lady's heart. Without looking to the right or left to notice the scene of rural wealth, on which he had so often gloated, he went straight to the stable, and with several hearty cuffs and kicks, roused his steed most uncourteously from the comfortable quarters in which he was soundly sleeping, dreaming of mountains of corn and oats, and whole valleys of timothy and clover.

Das Fest löste sich nun allmählich auf. Die alten Pächter luden die Ihrigen auf ihre Wagen, die man eine Zeitlang durch die Hohlwege und über die entfernten Hügel rasseln hörte. Einige Mädchen setzten sich auf Reitkissen hinter ihre Liebsten, und ihr unbeschwertes Lachen hallte, vermischt mit dem Hufgeklapper, in den stillen Wäldern wider, bis die immer schwächeren Töne allmählich verhallten – und der Schauplatz, den kurz vorher Lärm und Fröhlichkeit belebt hatten, still und verödet war. Ichabod allein blieb noch zurück, nach der Sitte der ländlichen Freier, um mit der Erbin ein Tête-à-Tête zu führen, in der vollen Überzeugung, nun auf dem geraden Wege zu seinem Glück zu sein.

Was sich bei diesem Gespräch begab, nehme ich mir nicht heraus zu erzählen, weil ich es in der Tat nicht weiß. Etwas muß jedoch, fürchte ich, schiefgegangen sein, da es gewiß ist, daß er sich nach kurzer Zeit mit untröstlicher Miene und langem Gesichte heimwärts wandte. O diese Frauen! Diese Frauen! Konnte es möglich sein, daß dieses Mädchen ihm einen ihrer koketten Streiche gespielt hatte? War ihre Aufmunterung des armen Schulmeisters nichts als eine Scharade, um ihr die Eroberung seines Nebenbuhlers zu sichern? Der Himmel weiß es, ich nicht. Nur so viel sage ich, Ichabod schlich sich davon und sah nicht ans, als ob er das Herz einer schönen Dame, nein, als ob er einen Hühnerkorb geplündert hätte. Ohne sich nach rechts oder links nach dem ländlichen Überflusse umzuschauen, worauf er so oft sehnsüchtig geblickt hatte, ging er schnurstracks in den Stall und weckte mit tüchtigen Stößen und Tritten sehr unhöflich sein Pferd aus der behaglichen Ruhe, worin es tief schlummerte und von ganzen Korn- und Haferbergen, von ganzen Tälern von Wiesengras und Klee träumte.

It was the very witching time of night that Ichabod, heavy-hearted and crest-fallen, pursued his travel homewards, along the sides of the lofty hills which rise above Tarry Town, and which he had traversed so cheerily in the afternoon. The hour was as dismal as himself. Far below him, the Tappaan Zee spread its dusky and indistinct waste of waters, with here and there the tall mast of a sloop, riding quietly at anchor under the land. In the dead hush of midnight, he could even hear the barking of the watch-dog from the opposite shore of the Hudson; but it was so vague and faint as only to give an idea of his distance from this faithful companion of man. Now and then, too, the long-drawn crowing of a cock, accidentally awakened, would sound far, far off, from some farm-house away among the hills—but it was like a dreaming sound in his ear. No signs of life occurred near him, but occasionally the melancholy chirp of a cricket, or perhaps the guttural twang of a bull-frog, from a neighbouring marsh, as if sleeping uncomfortably, and turning suddenly in his bed.

All the stories of ghosts and goblins that he had heard in the afternoon, now came crowding upon his recollection. The night grew darker and darker; the stars seemed to sink deeper in the sky, and driving clouds occasionally hid them from his sight. He had never felt so lonely and dismal.

He was, moreover, approaching the very place where many of the scenes of the ghost stories had been laid. In the centre of the road stood an enormous tulip tree, which towered like a giant above all the other trees of the neighbourhood, and formed a kind of land-mark.

Es war in der rechten Hexenstunde der Nacht, als Ichabod mit schwerem und betrübtem Herzen längs dem Abhange des Hügels heim ritt, der sich über Tarrytown erhebt, auf demselben Wege, den er am Nachmittage mit so frohem Gemüte gemacht hatte. Die Stunde war so trübselig wie er selbst. Tief unter ihm breitete der Tappaan-Zee ihre düstere wässrige Ebene in unbestimmter Dämmerung aus, wo hier und da der lange Mast einer Schaluppe emporragte, die ruhig unter dem hohen Uferlande vor Anker lag. In der totenstillen Mitternachtsstunde hörte er sogar das Gebelle des Hofhundes vom jenseitigen Ufer des Hudson, aber es war so schwach und unbestimmt, daß es nur eine Ahnung seiner Entfernung von dem getreuen Gefährten des Menschen erweckte. Zuweilen erschallte auch das langgedehnte Krähen eines zufällig erwachten Hahns aus irgend einem sehr weit entfernten Landgute im Gebirge, aber es klang nur wie ein Traumton in seinen Ohren. Kein Zeichen von Leben war in seiner Nähe, als von Zeit zu Zeit das traurige Zirpen einer Grille, oder vielleicht aus einem benachbarten Sumpfe der Kehlton eines Frosches, der etwa unruhig schlafen oder sich plötzlich in seinem Lager umwenden mochte.

Alle Geschichten von Geistern und Kobolden, die er am Nachmittag gehört hatte, drängten sich nun seiner Erinnerung auf. Die Nacht ward immer dunkler; die Sterne schienen immer tiefer in das Himmelsgewölbe zu sinken und treibende Wolken verbargen sie zuweilen vor seinen Blicken. Er hatte sich noch nie so einsam und traurig gefühlt.

Außerdem näherte er sich dem Orte, welcher der Schauplatz vieler Geistergeschichten gewesen war. Mitten auf der Straße stand ein ungeheurer Tulpenbaum, der sich wie ein Riese über alle benachbarten Bäume erhob, und eine Art von Landmarke bildete.

Its limbs were knarled, and fantastic, large enough to form trunks for ordinary trees, twisting down almost to the earth, and rising again into the air. It was connected with the tragical story of the unfortunate André, who had been taken prisoner hard by; and was universally known by the name of Major André's tree. The common people regarded it with a mixture of respect and superstition, partly out of sympathy for the fate of its ill-starred namesake, and partly from the tales of strange sights, and doleful lamentations told concerning it.

As Ichabod approached this fearful tree, he began to whistle: he thought his whistle was answered; it was but a blast sweeping sharply through the dry branches. As he approached a little nearer, he thought he saw something white, hanging in the midst of the tree; he paused and ceased whistling; but on looking more narrowly, perceived that it was a place where the tree had been scathed by lightning, and the white wood laid bare. Suddenly he heard a groan—his teeth chattered, and his knees smote against the saddle: it was but the rubbing of one huge bough upon another, as they were swayed about by the breeze. He passed the tree in safety, but new perils lay before him.

About two hundred yards from the tree a small brook crossed the road, and ran into a marshy and thickly wooded glen, known by the name of Wiley's swamp. A few rough logs, laid side by side, served for a bridge over this stream. On that side of the road where the brook entered the wood, a group of oaks and chestnuts, matted thick with wild grape vines, threw a cavernous gloom over it.

Seine Äste waren knorrig und bildeten phantastische Formen; dick genug für gewöhnliche Bäume, wanden sie sich beinahe bis auf die Erde herab, und stiegen dann wieder in die Luft empor. Der Baum ward in der Geschichte des unglücklichen André erwähnt, den man nahe dabei gefangen genommen hatte, und man nannte ihn überall Major André's Baum. Das gemeine Volk betrachtete ihn mit einer gemischten Regung von Ehrfurcht und Aberglauben, teils bewegt von Teilnahme mit dem Schicksale jenes armen Mannes, teils von der Erinnerung an die Geschichten von seltsamen Erscheinungen und traurigen Wehklagen, die man davon erzählte.

Als sich Ichabod dem furchtbaren Baume näherte, fing er an zu pfeifen. Er glaubte, sein Pfeifen wäre erwidert worden; aber es war nur ein Windstoß, der scharf durch die dürren Zweige blies. Er kam näher, und glaubte etwas Wießes mitten im Baum hängen zu sehen. Er hielt mit Pfeifen inne; als er aber genauer hinsah, fand er, daß es eine Stelle war, wo der Baum vom Blitz getroffen worden war, und das weiße Holz nackt hervorblickte. Plötzlich hörte er ein Stöhnen; seine Zähne klapperten, und seine Knie schlugen an den Sattel; aber es war nur ein mächtiger Zweig, der sich auf dem andern rieb, als der Wind sie bewegte. Er kam glücklich bei dem Baume vorüber, aber neue Gefahren lagen vor ihm.

Ungefähr dreihundert Schritte von dem Baume floß ein kleiner Bach über den Weg und strömte in ein sumpfiges, dicht beholztes Tal, das man Wiley's Sumpf nannte. Einige nebeneinander gelegte rohe Baumstämme dienten als Brücke. Auf der Seite des Weges, wo der Bach in den Wald floß, erhoben sich einige Eichen und Kastanienbäume, mit wilden Weinreben dicht durchflochten, die sich düster darüber wölbten.

To pass this bridge, was the severest trial. It was at this identical spot that the unfortunate André was captured, and under the covert of those chestnuts and vines were the sturdy yeomen concealed who surprised him. This has ever since been considered a haunted stream, and fearful are the feelings of the schoolboy who has to pass it alone after dark.

As he approached the stream, his heart began to thump; he summoned up, however, all his resolution, gave his horse half a score of kicks in the ribs, and attempted to dash briskly across the bridge; but instead of starting forward, the perverse old animal made a lateral movement, and ran broadside against the fence. Ichabod, whose fears increased with the delay, jerked the reins on the other side, and kicked lustily with the contrary foot: it was all in vain; his steed started, it is true, but it was only to plunge to the opposite side of the road into a thicket of brambles and elder bushes. The schoolmaster now bestowed both whip and heel upon the starveling ribs of old Gunpowder, who dashed forward, snuffling and snorting, but came to a stand just by the bridge with a suddenness that had nearly sent his rider sprawling over his head. Just at this moment a plashy tramp by the side of the bridge caught the sensitive ear of Ichabod. In the dark shadow of the grove, on the margin of the brook, he beheld something huge, misshapen, black and towering. It stirred not, but seemed gathered up in the gloom, like some gigantic monster ready to spring upon the traveller.

The hair of the affrighted pedagogue rose upon his head with terror. What was to be done? To turn and fly was now too late; and besides, what chance was there of escaping ghost or goblin, if such it was, which could ride upon the wings of the wind?

Über diese Brücke zu gehen, war die härteste Prüfung. An eben jener Stelle war der unglückliche André gefangen worden, und unter dem Schatten dieser Kastanienbäume und Reben waren die kräftigen Gegner, die ihn überfielen, verborgen gewesen. Seitdem war es an diesem Bache nicht geheuer, und jeder Schulknabe zitterte, der nach Anbruch der Dunkelheit diesen Weg gehen mußte.

Als er sich dem Bach näherte, begann sein Herz zu pochen; aber er nahm seine ganze Entschlossenheit zusammen, versetzte seinem Pferde mehrere Rippenstöße, und wollte rasch über die Brücke setzen. Das störrische alte Tier war jedoch nicht vorwärts zu bringen, sondern machte eine Bewegung zur Seite und rannte gerade gegen den Zaun. Ichabod, dessen Angst bei der Verzögerung stieg, riß die Zügel auf die andere Seite und stieß munter mit dem andern Fuße. Alles vergebens! Das Tier erschrak, sprang aber alsbald auf die andere Seite des Weges in ein Dickicht von Brombeergesträuch und Holunderbüschen. Ichabod gebrauchte nun Peitsche und Fersen gegen die mageren Rippen des alten Gunpowder, der keuchend und schnaubend voran schoß, aber so plötzlich gerade vor der Brücke stehen blieb, daß der Reiter ihm beinahe über den Kopf geflogen wäre. In diesem Augenblicke hörte Ichabods empfindliches Ohr ein Stampfen auf dem Moorboden nahe an der Brücke. Im dunklen Schatten des Gebüsches, am Rande des Baches, sah er eine ungeheure, schwarze, hochragende Mißgestalt. Sie bewegte sich nicht von der Stelle, schien sich aber aufzurichten in der Dunkelheit, wie ein Riesenungeheuer, im Begriff, auf den Reisenden loszuspringen.

Dem erschrockenen Schulmeister sträubte sich das Haar. Was sollte er tun? Um umzukehren und zu fliehen, war zu spät, und wie ließ sich einem Geiste oder Kobold entrinnen, wenn es ein solches Wesen war, das auf des Windes Flügeln daher fahren konnte?

Summoning up, therefore, a show of courage, he demanded in stammering accents— "Who are you?" He received no reply. He repeated his demand in a still more agitated voice. —Still there was no answer. Once more he cudgelled the sides of the inflexible Gunpowder, and shutting his eyes, broke forth with involuntary fervour into a psalm tune. Just then the shadowy object of alarm put itself in motion, and with a scramble and a bound, stood at once in the middle of the road. Though the night was dark and dismal, yet the form of the unknown might now in ... some degree be ascertained. He appeared to be a horseman of large dimensions, and mounted on a black horse of powerful frame. He made no offer of molestation or sociability, but kept aloof on one side of the road, jogging along on the blind side of old Gunpowder, who had now got over his fright and waywardness.

Ichabod, who had no relish for this strange midnight companion, and bethought himself of the adventure of Brom Bones with the Galloping Hessian, now quickened his steed, in hopes of leaving him behind. The stranger, however, quickened his horse to an equal pace. Ichabod pulled up, and fell into a walk, thinking to lag behind—the other did the same. His heart began to sink within him; he endeavoured to resume his psalm tune, but his parched tongue clove to the roof of his mouth, and he could not utter a stave. There was something in the moody and dogged silence of this pertinacious companion, that was mysterious and appalling. It was soon fearfully accounted for.

Er nahm seinen ganzen Mut zusammen und fragte stammelnd: „Wer seid Ihr?" Keine Antwort. Er wiederholte die Frage mit noch aufgeregterer Stimme. Aber vergebens, niemand antwortete. Noch einmal peitschte er den unbeugsamen Gunpowder, und seine Augen schließend, brach er mit unwillkürlicher Inbrunst in eine Psalmenmelodie aus. In diesem Augenblick aber hatte die Schattengestalt sich in Bewegung gesetzt, und war mit einem Satz mitten auf dem Wege. So finster und furchtbar die Nacht auch war, so ließ sich doch die Gestalt des Unbekannten nun einigermaßen unterscheiden. Es schien ein gewaltiger Reiter auf einem mächtigen schwarzen Pferd zu sein. Er verriet keine Absicht, ihn zu belästigen oder sich zu ihm zu gesellen, sondern hielt Abstand auf der anderen Seite des Weges, und trabte auf der blinden Seite des alten Gunpowder, der nun seine Furcht und Bösartigkeit abgelegt hatte.

Ichabod, dem der seltsame mitternächtliche Gefährte nicht behagte, und der an Knochen-Broms Abenteuer mit dem galoppierenden Hessen dachte, trieb nun sein Roß an, in der Hoffnung, ihn hinter sich zu lassen. Der Unbekannte ritt gleichfalls schneller. Ichabod ließ sein Pferd in einen gemächlichen Schritt fallen, um zurückzubleiben – doch der andere tat es ihm gleich. Dem Schulmeister sank der Mut. Er suchte wieder seinen Psalm anzustimmen, aber seine ausgedorrte Zunge klebte an seinem Gaumen und er konnte keinen Vers herausbringen. Das finstere und verdrießliche Schweigen seines hartnäckigen Gefährten hatte etwas Geheimnisvolles und Erschreckendes an sich, und es wurde bald auf furchtbare Weise erklärt.

On mounting a rising ground, which brought the figure of his fellow traveller in relief against the sky, gigantic in height, and muffled in a cloak, Ichabod was horror-struck, on perceiving that he was headless!—but his horror was still more increased, on observing that the head, which should have rested on his shoulders, was carried before him on the pommel of the saddle! his terror rose to desperation; he rained a shower of kicks and blows upon Gunpowder, hoping, by a sudden movement, to give his companion the slip—but the spectre started full jump with him. Away then they dashed, through thick and thin; stones flying, and sparks flashing, at every bound. Ichabod's flimsy garments fluttered in the air, as he stretched his long lank body away over his horse's head, in the eagerness of his flight.

They had now reached the road which turns off to Sleepy Hollow; but Gunpowder, who seemed possessed with a demon, instead of keeping up it, made an opposite turn, and plunged headlong down hill to the left. This road leads through a sandy hollow, shaded by trees for about a quarter of a mile, where it crosses the bridge famous in goblin story, and just beyond swells the green knoll on which stands the whitewashed church.

As yet the panic of the steed had given his unskilful rider an apparent advantage in the chase; but just as he had got half way through the hollow, the girths of the saddle gave way, and he felt it slipping from under him. He seized it by the pommel, and endeavoured to hold it firm, but in vain; and had just time to save himself by clasping old Gunpowder round the neck, when the saddle fell to the earth, and he heard it trampled under foot by his pursuer.

Als sie eine Anhöhe erreichten, wo sich die Gestalt des riesengroßen, in einen Mantel gehüllten Reiters vor dem dunklen Himmelsgewölbe abzeichnete, sah Ichabod mit Entsetzen, daß sein Begleiter kopflos war, und sein Schrecken stieg noch höher, als er sah, daß der Kopf, der auf den Schultern hätte sitzen sollen, vor ihm auf dem Sattelknauf saß! Sein Entsetzen stieg bis zur Verzweiflung. Er ließ Stöße und Hiebe auf Gunpowder regnen, und hoffte durch eine plötzliche Bewegung seinem Begleiter zu entrinnen, aber das Gespenst blieb an seiner Seite. Fort ging es durch Dick und Dünn, und Steine flogen und Funken stoben bei jedem Satz. Ichabods fadenscheinige Kleider flatterten in der Luft, als er in der Eile der Flucht seinen langen dürren Leib über den Kopf des Pferdes streckte.

Sie hatten nun die Straße erreicht, die nach Sleepy Hollow führt, aber Gunpowder schien von einem Dämon besessen zu sein, und statt jenem Wege zu folgen, wendete sich das Tier auf die andere Seite und stürmte bergab. Dieser Pfad führt durch einen sandigen Hohlweg und ist eine Viertelmeile weit mit Bäumen beschattet, bis zu der in der Gespenstergeschichte berüchtigten Brücke, und gleich jenseits des Weges erhebt sich der grüne Hügel, worauf die weißgetünchte Kirche steht.

Der plötzliche Schrecken des Pferdes hatte dem unge-schickten Reiter einen scheinbaren Vorteil im Wettrennen gegeben, als er aber mitten im Hohlwege war, fühlte er, daß der Sattel, dessen Gurt sich gelöst hatte, unter ihm wegglitt. Er versuchte, den Sattel am Knauf festzuhalten, aber ver-gebens, und er hatte nur so viel Zeit, den Hals des alten Gunpowder zu umschlingen, um sich zu retten, als der Sattel auf die Erde fiel, und alsbald von seinem Verfolger niedergetreten wurde.

For a moment the terror of Hans Van Ripper's wrath passed across his mind—for it was his Sunday saddle; but this was no time for petty fears; the goblin was hard on his haunches; and (unskilful rider that he was he had much ado to maintain his seat; sometimes slipping on one side, sometimes on another, and sometimes jolted on the high ridge of his horse's back bone, with a violence that he verily feared would cleave him asunder.

An opening in the trees now cheered him with the hopes that the church bridge was at hand. The wavering reflection of a silver star in the bosom of the brook told him that he was not mistaken. He saw the walls of the church dimly glaring under the trees beyond. He recollected the place where Brom Bones' ghostly competitor had disappeared. "If I can but reach that bridge," thought Ichabod, "I am safe." Just then he heard the black steed panting and blowing close behind him; he even fancied that he felt his hot breath. Another convulsive kick in the ribs, and old Gunpowder sprung upon the bridge; he thundered over the resounding planks; he gained the opposite side; and now Ichabod cast a look behind to see if his pursuer should vanish, according to rule, in a flash of fire and brimstone. Just then he saw the goblin rising in his stirrups, and in the very act of hurling his head at him. Ichabod endeavoured to dodge the horrible missile, but too late. It encountered his cranium with a tremendous crash—he was tumbled headlong into the dust, and Gunpowder, the black steed, and the goblin rider, passed by like a whirl wind.

Für einen Augenblick durchfuhr ihn der erschreckende Gedanke an Hans Van Rippers Zorn, denn es war sein Sonntagsattel; aber es war nicht Zeit, so unbedeutenden Besorgnissen Raum zu geben. Das Gespenst war ihm dicht auf den Fersen, und er, der ungeschickte Reiter, hatte seine Not, sich auf seinem Sitze zu halten, da er bald auf die eine, bald auf die andre Seite glitt, und zuweilen mit einer Heftigkeit auf das hohe Rückgrat seines Pferdes stieß, daß er fürchtete, gespalten zu werden.

Eine Öffnung zwischen den Bäumen weckte in ihm nun die erfreuliche Hoffnung, daß die Kirchenbrücke nahe war. Der Widerschein eines blinkenden Sternes im Spiegel des Baches gab ihm die Bestätigung. Er sah die Mauern der Kirche unter den Bäumen matt hervorblinken. Et erinnerte sich an die Stelle, wo Knochen-Broms gespenstischer Gefährte verschwunden war. „Kann ich nur die Brücke erreichen", dachte Ichabod, „so bin ich in Sicherheit." In diesem Augenblicke aber hörte er den Rappen dicht hinter sich keuchen und schnauben, und er glaubte sogar des Tieres heißen Atem zu fühlen. Noch ein krampfhafter Stoß in die Rippen, und Gunpowder setzte über die Brücke, flog donnernd über die wiederhallenden Bohlen, und kam ans jenseitige Ufer. Ichabod warf nun einen Blick rückwärts, um zu sehen, ob sein Verfolger, der Regel gemäß, in einem Aufblitzen aus Feuer und Schwefel verschwände. In diesem Augenblicke aber erhob sich das Gespenst in den Steighügeln, und war im Begriff, seinen Kopf auf ihn zu schleudern. Ichabod versuchte, dem furchtbaren Wurfgeschoß auszuweichen, aber zu spät! Es traf seinen Schädel mit entsetzlichem Krachen; er stürzte in den Staub und Gunpowder, der Rappe und das Reitergespenst flogen wie ein Wirbelwind an ihm vorüber.

The next morning the old horse was found without his saddle, and with the bridle under his feet, soberly cropping the grass at his master's gate. Ichabod did not make his appearance at breakfast —dinner-hour came, but no Ichabod. The boys assembled at the schoolhouse, and strolled idly about the banks of the brook; but no schoolmaster. Hans Van Ripper now began to feel some uneasiness about the fate of poor Ichabod, and his saddle. An inquiry was set on foot, and after diligent in vestigation they came upon his traces. In one part of the road leading to the church, was found the saddle trampled in the dirt; the tracks of horses' hoofs deeply dented in the road, and evidently at furious speed, were traced to the bridge, beyond which, on the bank of a broad part of the brook, where the water ran deep and black, was found the hat of the unfortunate Ichabod, and close beside it a shattered pumpkin.

The brook was searched, but the body of the schoolmaster was not to be discovered. Hans Van Ripper, as executor of his estate, examined the bundle which contained all his worldly effects, They consisted of two shirts and a half; two stocks for the neck; a pair or two of worsted stockings; an old pair of corduroy small-clothes; a rusty razor; a book of psalm tunes, full of dog's ears; and a broken pitch-pipe. As to the books and furniture of the schoolhouse, they belonged to the community, excepting Cotton Mather's History of Witchcraft, a New-England Almanack, and a book of dreams and fortune-telling; in which last was a sheet of foolscap much scribbled and blotted in several fruitless attempts to make a copy of verses in honour of the heiress of Van Tassel.

Am nächsten Morgen fand man das Pferd ohne Sattel, mit dem Zaume unter den Füßen, ehrbar grasend vor der Türe seines Herrn. Ichabod erschien nicht beim Frühstück; die Tischzeit kam, aber kein Ichabod. Die Knaben versammelten sich im Schulhaus und schlenderten müßig am Bachlauf entlang, aber kein Schulmeister ließ sich sehen. Hans Van Ripper wurde nun ein wenig besorgt um den armen Ichabod, und um seinen Sattel. Man stellte Nachforschungen an, und nach eifriger Untersuchung entdeckte man seine Spur. Auf der Straße, die zur Kirche führte, fand man den Sattel in den Dreck getreten; man konnte tief eingedrückte Spuren von Pferdehufen, die offenbar in willder Eile geflogen waren, bis zur Brücke verfolgen, und jenseits derselben, am Ufer, wo der breitere Bach tief und dunkel floß, lag der Hut des unglücklichen Ichabod und nicht weit davon ein zerborstener Kürbis.

Der Bach wurde untersucht, aber der Leichnam des Schulmeisters wurde nicht gefunden. Hans Van Ripper, als Aufseher des Nachlasses, untersuchte das Bündel, worin sich Ichabods gesamte weltliche Besitztümer befanden. Sie bestand in zweieinhalb Hemden, zwei Halsbinden, ein oder zwei Paar Kammgarnstrümpfen, einem alten Paar gerippter Unterhosen, einem rostigen Schermesser, einem eselsohrigen Psalmenbuch und einer zerbrochenen Stimmpfeife. Die Bücher und das Gerät im Schulhaus waren Eigentum der Gemeinde, ausgenommen Cotton Mather's Geschichte der Hexerei, ein Kalender von Neu-England, sowie auch ein Traum- und Wahrsage-Buch, worin auf einem feinem wießen Blatt viel gekritzelt und ausgestrichen war, bei vergeblichen Versuchen, einige Verse zu Ehren der Van Tassel-Erbin ins Reine zu schreiben.

These magic books and the poetic scrawl were forthwith consigned to the flames by Hans Van Ripper; who from that time forward determined to send his children no more to school; observing, that he never knew any good come of this same reading and writing. Whatever money the schoolmaster possessed, and he had received his quarter's pay but a day or two before, he must have had about his person at the time of his disappearance.

The mysterious event caused much speculation at the church on the following Sunday. Knots of gazers and gossips were collected in the church yard, at the bridge, and at the spot where the hat and pumpkin had been found. The stories of Brouwer, of Bones, and a whole budget of others, were called to mind; and when they had diligently considered them all, and compared them with the symptoms of the present case, they shook their heads, and came to the conclusion that Ichabod had been carried off by the galloping Hessian. As he was a bachelor, and in nobody's debt, nobody troubled his head anymore about him; the school was removed to a different quarter of the hollow, and another pedagogue reigned in his stead.

Dieses Buch samt dem poetischen Gekritzel übergab Hans Van Ripper sogleich den Flammen, und faßte den Entschluß, seine Kinder fortan nicht mehr in die Schule zu schicken, mit der Bemerkung, er wüßte nicht, wie aus solcher Leserei und Schreiberei irgend etwas Gutes kommen könnte. Was der Schulmeister an Geld besessen haben mochte – und es war ihm erst zwei Tage vorher seine vierteljährige Besoldung ausgezahlt worden – mußte er zur Zeit seines Verschwindens bei sich gehabt haben.

Das mysteriöse Ereignis löste am folgenden Sonntag beim Kirchgang viele Spekulationen aus. Es sammelten sich Haufen von Gaffern und Schwätzern auf dem Kirchhof, an der Brücke und auf der Stelle, wo man Hut und Kürbis gefunden hatte. Man rief sich die Geschichten von Brouwer, Knochen-Brom und allen anderen zurück, und als man alle sorgfältig erwogen und mit den Erscheinungen des vorliegenden Falles verglichen hatte, schüttelte man den Kopf und kam zu dem Schluß, der galoppierende Hesse hätte den Schulmeister entführt. Ichabod war ein Junggeselle und niemanden etwas schuldig, daher bekümmerte sich niemand mehr um ihn; die Schule wurde in eine andere Gegend des Tales verlegt, und ein anderer Lehrer übernahm die Leitung.

It is true, an old farmer, who had been down to NewYork on a visit several years after, and from whom this account of the ghostly adventure was received, brought home the intelligence that Ichabod Crane was still alive; that he had left the neighbourhood partly through fear of the goblin and Hans Van Ripper, and partly in mortification at having been suddenly dismissed by the heiress; that he had changed his quarters to a distant part of the country; had kept school and studied law at the same time; had been admitted to the bar, turned politician, electioneered, written for the newspapers, and finally had been made a justice of the Ten Pound Court. Brom Bones too, who shortly after his rival's disappearance conducted the blooming Katrina in triumph to the altar, was observed to look exceedingly knowing whenever the story of Ichabod was related, and always burst into a hearty laugh at the mention of the pumpkin; which led some to suspect that he knew more about the matter than he chose to tell.

The old country wives, however, who are the best judges of these matters, maintain to this day, that Ichabod was spirited away by supernatural means; and it is a favourite story often told about the neighbourhood round the winter evening fire. The bridge became more than ever an object of superstitious awe, and that may be the reason why the road has been altered of late years, so as to approach the church by the border of the mill-pond. The schoolhouse being deserted, soon fell to decay, and was reported to be haunted by the ghost of the unfortunate pedagogue; and the ploughboy, loitering homeward of a still summer evening, has often fancied his voice at a distance, chanting a melancholy psalm tune among the tranquil solitudes of Sleepy Hollow.

Ein alter Landmann, der mehre Jahre später nach New York reiste, der Erzähler dieser Gespenstergeschichte, brachte die Nachricht mit, daß Ichabod Crane noch lebte, daß er seinen früheren Wohnort teils aus Furcht vor dem Gespenst und vor Hans Van Ripper, teils aus Verdruß über den so plötzlich von der Erbin erhaltenen Korb verlassen, daß er in einer entlegenen Gegend des Landes seinen Wohnsitz genommen, eine Schule geführt und dabei gleichzeitig die Rechtswissenschaft erlernt und schließlich als Advokat zugelassen wurde, darauf Politiker und Wahlhelfer, Zeitungschreiber und zuletzt gar Friedensrichter geworden war. Knochen-Brom, der bald nach dem Verschwinden seines Nebenbuhlers die blühende Katrina in stolzer Siegesfreude zum Altar geführt hatte, sah sehr pfiffig aus, so oft Ichabods Geschichte erzählt wurde, und bei Erwähnung des Kürbisses brach er immer in ein herzliches Gelächter aus, was manche auf den Argwohn brachte, daß ihm mehr von der Geschichte bekannt wäre, als ihm zu sagen beliebte.

Die alten Bauernweiber aber, die am besten über solche Dinge zu urteilen verstehen, behaupten bis auf den heutigen Tag, Ichabod wäre auf übernatürliche Weise verschwunden, und es ist eine Lieblingsgeschichte, die man gern abends am winterlichen Herde erzählt. Die Brücke ward mehr als je ein Gegenstand abergläubischer Furcht, und dies mag die Ursache gewesen sein, daß man seither den Weg zur Kirche längs dem Mühlteiche angelegt hat. Das verlassene Schulhaus geriet bald in Verfall, und der unglückliche Schulmeister sollte darin umgehen, und wenn der Ackerjunge an einem stillen Sommerabende heimschlenderte, glaubte er oft Ichabods Stimme in der Ferne zu hören, wie sie in der ruhigen Einsamkeit von Sleepy Hollow eine traurige Psalmenmelodie sang.

The preceding Tale is given, almost in the precise words in which I heard it related at a Corporation meeting of the ancient city of the Manhattoes,[12] at which were present many of its sagest and most illustrious burghers. The narrator was a pleasant, shabby, gentlemanly old fellow, in pepper-and-salt clothes, with a sadly humorous face; and one whom I strongly suspected of being poor, —he made such efforts to be entertaining. When his story was concluded, there was much laughter and approbation, particularly from two or three deputy alder men, who had been asleep the greater part of the time. There was, however, one tall, dry-looking, old gentle man, with beetling eyebrows, who maintained a grave and rather severe face throughout: now and then folding his arms, inclining his head, and looking down upon the floor, as if turning a doubt over in his mind. He was one of your wary men, who never laugh, but upon good grounds—when they have reason and the law on their side. When the mirth of the rest of the company had subsided, and silence was restored, he leaned one arm on the elbow of his chair, and sticking the other akimbo, demanded, with a slight, but exceedingly sage motion of the head, and contraction of the brow, what was the moral of the story, and what it went to prove?

---

[12] New York.

Vorstehende Geschichte ist fast in denselben Worten wiedergegeben worden, wie ich sie bei einer Versammlung in der alten Stadt der Manhottoes[13] erzählen hörte, wobei viele der klügsten und angesehensten Bürger zugegen waren. Der Erzähler war ein freundlicher, artiger Mann, jedoch ein wenig ärmlich in einen graumelierte Anzug gekleidet, mit einem trübselig launigen Gesichte, ein Mann, den ich für bedürftig hielt, weil er sich so viel Mühe gab, unterhaltsam zu sein. Als er seine Geschichte geendigt hatte, gab es viel Gelächter und Beifallsbezeigungen, besonders von Seiten einiger Ratsherren, welche die meiste Zeit geschlafen hatten. Es befand sich jedoch unter den Anwesenden ein sehr trocken aussehender alter Herr mit buschigen Augenbrauen, der während der ganzen Erzählung ein ernstes, fast finsteres Gesicht machte, zuweilen seine Arme verschränkte, den Kopf neigte, und auf den Boden blickte, als ob er einen Zweifel erwogen hätte. Es war einer jener argwöhnischen Menschen, die nur aus guten Gründen lachen, wenn sie die Vernunft und das Recht auf ihrer Seite haben. Als die Heiterkeit der übrigen Anwesenden nachgelassen hatte und alles wieder schwieg, stützte er einen Arm auf die Stuhllehne und stemmte den andern in die Seite, und fragte er mit einer leichten, aber ungemein klugen Kopfbewegung, und zusammengezogenen Brauen, welche Lehre denn aus der Geschichte gezogen werden, und was sie beweisen sollte.

---

[13] New York, von dem Namen des Stammes der amerikanischen Ureinwohner, die hier einst ihren Sitz hatten.

The story-teller, who was just putting a glass of wine to his lips, as a refreshment after his toils, paused for a moment, looked at his inquirer with an air of infinite deference, and lowering the glass slowly to the table, observed, that the story was intended most logically to prove: "That there is no situation in life but has its advantages and pleasures—provided we will but take a joke as we find it: "That, therefore, he that runs races with goblin troopers, is likely to have rough riding of it: "Ergo, for a country schoolmaster to be refused the hand of a Dutch heiress, is a certain step to high preferment in the state."

The cautious old gentleman knit his brows tenfold closer after this explanation, being sorely puzzled by the ratiocination of the syllogism; while, methought, the one in pepper-and-salt eyed him with something of a triumphant leer. At length, he observed, that all this was very well, but still he thought the story a little on the extravagant—there were one or two points on which he had his doubts.

"Faith, Sir," replied the story-teller, "as to that matter, I don't believe one half of it myself."

Der Erzähler, der eben ein Glas Wein zum Munde führte, um sich nach seiner Anstrengung zu erfrischen, schwieg einen Augenblick, blickte dann mit ungemeiner Ehrerbietung auf den Frager, und bemerkte, das Glas langsam niedersetzend: „Daß die Geschichte sehr bündig beweisen sollte, daß keine Lebenslage ohne ihre Vorteile und Freuden wäre, wenn wir nur mit einem Scherze hinein gingen; daß daher derjenige, der mit gespenstischen Reitern ein Wettrennen hielte, vermutlich sehr übel fahren möchte, und folglich ein Landschulmeister, der von einer niederländischen Erbin einen Korb bekäme, auf dem sichersten Wege wäre, zu hohen Würden im Staate zu kommen."

Der wachsame alte Herr zog nach dieser Erläuterung die Stirne noch zehnmal mehr zusammen, und die Schlußfolgerung setzte ihn nicht wenig in Verwirrung, während der Mann im graumelierten Anzug ihn beinahe triumphierend ansah. Endlich machte jener die Bemerkung, alles dies wäre gut und schön, aber die Geschichte käme ihm doch ein wenig übertrieben vor, und besonders über zwei Punkte hätte er seine Zweifel.

„Ja freilich", erwiderte der Erzähler, „wollen wir davon reden, so glaube ich selber nicht mehr als die Hälfte davon."